THE ON-PURPOSE CEO PRESENTS:

Bigger
Business
Blueprint

MODERN MARKETING, INNOVATION & SCALABLE GROWTH

BY JASON PALLISER

Eva + Peter,
Can't wait to
see your bigger
business blueprint
Jason Palliser

.

Copyright © 2016 by Jason Palliser

ISBN 978-0-9910416-7-1 (Print)

Table of Contents

Acknowledgements

First I want to thank my family for helping me get this transformative book to the finish line. Thanks to my wife Jacki Palliser for keeping the household running smoothly while I typed away, feverishly trying to finish. Thanks to Sydney and Gracie for helping with baby Eva during the home stretch of the book. Reed, thanks for halfway staying out of trouble. You guys and gals are my daily motivation, my inspiration to work harder, and to provide value to all that come into the Bigger Business Blueprint fold.

Thank you to some of the special people I do business with (now or in the past). You have each shaped my tireless pursuit for business perfection (some will be surprised they made an impact, but you did). Your honest feedback was invaluable to the successful completion of the book. I'd like to thank Bryan Wynn, Casey Eberhart, Alicia Sierra, Blake Adams, Jason Lucchesi, Miles Kallial, Maite Webster, Deanna Rogers, Caren Glasser, Brian Hanson, Greg Schowe, Greig Wells, Randy Delkus, Joseph Pagano Jr., Aaron Barnes, Brad Sides, Shaun McCloskey, John Palliser, Terry Yuede, Keith Yuede, Ruben Perez, Jonathan Dugger, Vince Johnson, Dwayne Johnson, Knox Mailhes, Dave Vanhoose, Bernard Ablola, David Fagan, Jarin Giesler, Greg Russell, Sam Bell, Rhonda Phillips, Adrian Lyew, Keavin Blount, John Swiercinsky, Gary Ott, Travis Howard, Todd Duncan, Doug Stahlschmidt, Bill Hart, Nick Baur, Kevin Short, Francis Ablola, Jimena Cortez, Alex Tillman, Stephen Carleson, Jamie Kerestes, Cory Boatright, Dolmar Cross and Allie Pasag. There are many more, so thank you to everyone who has participated. You all had a role in shaping the final product, whether it was your passion, philosophy, follow through, the ability to say no, innovation, persistence, mind, principal, integrity, and much more.

Thank you to a few of my consulting clients, business leaders, and collaborators who helped participate in fine-tuning the book's focus and large impact takeaways. To name a few... Affinity Real Estate Investment Company, Elite Legacy, Lifestyles Unlimited, Digital Marketer, Expand The Business, World Care Alliance, Medical Recovery Services, Medical Management Services, Bank of Sullivan, Resolutions Title, REI BlackBook, Real Market Masters, Flipping Formula, Promote Your Passion, Rich Dad Education, Lifeonaire, The Yuede Team, Giesler Sports World Wide, Success Team Marketing Group, Planet Rent To Own, and many more. Thank you for your support!

-Jason Palliser

Introduction

Growing your business in the fast-paced, ever-changing landscape of the consumer marketplace is a difficult task. It demands honesty about your company's current position. It insists on dedication and a willingness to learn new strategies. It requires that you commit to growing your business with purposeful and deliberate action. This is no easy feat.

All too often, I engage business owners that know they need to create strategic growth for their company, but simply get stuck in what I affectionately call the, *"This is what has worked for me in the past!"* business owner-trap. Most business owners plug away, the way they have always "done it," and keep themselves from strategic growth and success. This book delivers a <u>Bigger</u> <u>Business Blueprint</u> to become a more profitable *Modern Business* that commands growth that is "On-Purpose" and no longer "By Accident!"

You see, there is such a thing in business as *accidental-growth*, where due to no strategic planning from the business owner, they become a little more profitable (which all business owners like), but they cannot for the life of them put their *business-finger* on "how or why" they have had an increase in sales. I think we all know this is not a sustainable model, especially with new competitors popping up (seemingly overnight) to try and take a piece of our free-enterprise pie. The fact is that most business owners go through periods of growth and decline.

After all, that is the nature of business in a free competitive market.

All of us love growth, but we just need to make sure it is _purposeful growth_ or _on-purpose growth_ that we can quantify and grow from, instead of _accidental-growth._ Accidental growth is dangerous because market pressures can swing the profit pendulum in a negative direction, and without purposeful-growth plans in place, that pendulum can erode a business owner's company in short order.

This book should serve as your Bigger Business Blueprint to _on-purpose growth_ to help your business be more profitable in today's modern, fast-paced marketplace.

As we start to construct your Bigger Business Blueprint you will begin to clearly see the income possibilities for your business. The key element in attaining this 21st century style of profitable and nimble business is _deliberate, purposeful planning_ that is spurred on by modern marketplace efficiencies that most business CEOs don't know exist. The biggest blueprint advantage we will infuse into your business is effortless tracking that gives you unmatched business intelligence to make smart business building decisions, backed by data, to eliminate accidental growth. We will seed these modern business _non-negotiables_ into your marketing, your brand building, your customer maximization plan, and your business standard practices to drop the competition to their knees. We will begin to pull your business away from accidental growth, move towards on-purpose growth, and even faster on-purpose wealth. The blueprint to the bigger business you deserve lays within these carefully constructed pages. So let's move from accidental to on purpose growth!

Some examples of accidental-growth is when a competitor goes out of business, raises their prices, or moves. Typically the problem with this growth is that it is hard to bottle up or quantify because there was no real purposeful business planning put behind it. Without sustainable growth plans, and in an ever-changing business environment, business owners face the ups and downs of business profitability.

Building a Bigger Business Blueprint is an endeavor that every entrepreneur seeks to master. The cold hard fact is that the pursuit for business nirvana is a never-ending journey. Therefore, the pursuit for a bigger business should be one that develops a blueprint for triggering systematic growth. This is achieved by infusing business non-negotiables that poise any business for increased productivity and profitability. By attacking business growth with an "On-Purpose" approach, you can begin to lay the framework for a Bigger Business Blueprint and improve marketing, sales and profitability.

Being in business for approaching 22 years, and touching thousands of business owners through speaking and training nationally on marketing, branding, and productivity; I have found a pattern of growth inhibitors that plague most business owners. Whether I'm hired to perform business consulting or contracted by large companies to teach entrepreneur workshops, I find that entrepreneurs are desperate to grow their businesses, but are lost in the never-ending sea of to-do items that leave most feeling frustrated and wondering where the money went.

Bigger Business Blueprint is a compilation of developed non-negotiable business building principles, sharpened from every business owner I have impacted throughout my professional career. It delivers to you as the CEO Entrepreneur, the ability to see the clearest vision of what your business can become. It will illuminate the clearest path to getting out of your own way - allowing for purposeful growth that is infused with undeniable brand-building, marketing weapons, and modern hands-free growth blueprints that will smash the competition.

Designing a modern business that embraces the 21st century free-marketplace and embodies "On-Purpose Growth" includes strategic planning and implementation of the sales and marketing strategies. A well-designed modern business is poised to stand the test of business-time, and is nimble enough to take on the changes that lie ahead, while profiting along the way.

THE COLD HARD BUSINESS FACTS!

If it is a fact, then let's face it. The cold hard business fact is that the Internet is a 24/7 pipeline directly into the information and technology highway. Consumers look to get what they want, when they want it, and like to get it right now with as little guesswork and uncertainty as they can; they turn to the Internet to do it. Consumers don't want product options in months, weeks or days, they want them in seconds and your business better be ready to deliver. Today's consumers want instant answers, even if they may not be ready to buy for weeks or months. They still demand information now! (Whether it means looking up product reviews, finding an online menu, or doing background research on a company.) Business owners today need to address the eight hundred pound gorilla in the room, which is that consumers rely on the Internet heavily to solve their problems and they want it in seconds, versus weeks or months.

So where does that put us today? Consumers want everything now, so one of the big-ticket business items to identify is how to modernize our business to meet the consumers demand online (where they live and breathe). Whether it is on their phones, computers or other Internet driven devices, we have to have our brand meet them on their purchasing turf. Doesn't it make sense? If consumers want products and services 24/7, then shouldn't your products and services be on display 24/7?

Of course they should.

Modernizing your business and business practices to attack 21st century buyer demands are monster steps in the right business direction. One way to make sure you are up for the business-owner-challenge is to make sure that you always remember that you have COMPETITION and they want to take market share away from you. It is your job as the CEO of your business to make sure that you build a 21st century business that is conscious of the competition and ready for the on-demand consumer marketplace challenge.

The silverlining here is that with the advent of the information and technology highway, your business can become an instant star with leveraged automation weapons. Better yet, become a profitability monster by making sure you meet everyone where they consume (online) and make sure that your business brand is always around every consumer turn, to cement your top-of-mind awareness.

MODERNIZING

As we dive into modernizing your business, we will look at your process for improvement and look at your team (or lack of one) for measurable improvement. We will look for revenue diversification (which is easier than ever in today's marketplace) and look to make your business maximize revenue potential like never before. Since consumers seemingly have an endless supply of choices today, it is our job to simply become the logical choice for your products and services. This is accomplished through marketing, branding, and sales principles that help you transform into the most profitable modern business you can become, while streamlining business efficiencies that drive revenue growth even higher.

If we all agree where we stand in today's marketplace, then what are we going to do about it? Some business owners ignore the changing business environment and continue to eat stress for breakfast, lunch, and dinner. Sticking your business-head in the sand is not an "On-Purpose Business" option! Of course not! You are here to become a bigger business. That already shows me that you are not ready to give up or give in. It shows me that you are ready to fight for your piece of the entrepreneur pie.

I hear all of the time, from hundreds of business owners that I consult with and teach, the following phrases:

- I don't know where to start? (Start here!)
- Things are so different now, so I guess time has passed me by! (No it hasn't!)
- I am not technical! (You don't need to be!)
- Well, those aren't my customers. They are not online! (Yes, they are!)

Here is the truth. When I hear these words come out of entrepreneurs' mouths, I believe them. I believe them because they have never taken the steps to push their business forward and see what is really out there for the taking by stepping out of their daily grind and comfort zone. More over, they have not actually made the CEO decision to roll up their sleeves and say, "It is time for me to do what I need to do to take and keep the marketshare I deserve and become a 21st century business!" Through the course of this training, we are going to build your Bigger Business Blueprint together by simply reverse engineering your best on-purpose business.

Any business can grow and be more profitable. We just need to start asking the right questions, identifying strengths and weaknesses, while putting a business growth plan in place to execute your new business-vision. The typical business problem is that most business owners and/or CEOs get pulled in fifty different directions that are not High-Dollar-Money-Making-Activities, which robs them of the opportunity of purposefully working on growth. Through dissecting your business to its core, we take steps towards impactful change *On-Purpose* and *Not-by-Accident*! That is what CEOs who want to grow their businesses do! <u>They build purposeful businesses</u>!

Your business deserves a blueprint comprised of modern growth non-negotiables, winning marketing formulas, sales performance non-negotiables, and lock-n-load automatic growth tools. Combined in the world's best business execution blueprint, you will command expected growth, embrace new efficiency, and remove yourself from the business-trenches to watch your business thrive from the sidelines - with you as the biggest cheerleader.

Chapter 1:

To Know Your Business, Is To Grow Your Business!

GETTING INTIMATE WITH YOUR BUSINESS!
[DEVELOPING YOUR BUSINESS HONESTY SCORE]

To know your business, is to grow your business! Time to get intimate with your business! Your business is just like a personal relationship. It has strengths and weaknesses. To grow your business purposefully, we first need to identify areas of strength and areas of weakness. The best way to achieve this is to get intimate with your business.

Getting intimate can deliver great joy, but it also can be uncomfortable if we are not rock solid or unsure where we stand. It only starts to feel good when we truly know where we stand and we are confident we have put our best foot forward - and the same goes for your personal relationship with your business. The only way to be on solid ground is to start with honesty! That's where you are marching; straight towards _business honesty_, so you have the best chance to grow.

Just like growing a stronger relationship, you need the same honest evaluation to see where you are with your business and more importantly, where it needs to go based upon your assessment. Typically, this is the hardest item to do because more often than not, the truth hurts. For some, living in a state of denial is easier because whether things are good or not, denial about where you currently are (in relationships or in business) at least gets you a little further down the road.

The honest truth though is that unless you take time to evaluate, you may not see the road is a dead end. It is only months or years later that you realize the folly and that lost time makes it even harder to get back on the right path. Avoiding pain and discomfort today creates further pain down the line and postpones achieving bigger business and personal growth. After all, doesn't the old saying ring true? "The truth shall set you free!" It is time to put your business mind to work to help you grab what you deserve: growth!

BUSINESS FACT: EVERY BUSINESS CAN IMPROVE!

We all can improve. Think about it. If we can't improve, then you are stuck where you are because that is the best you're going to be. Absurd, right? Of course it is! So let's transform your business forever. The best way to achieve business improvement is to dissect and identify areas of business strength and weakness, in order to build the path to your best business! It is a fact that most people will achieve more when they are placed in an atmosphere where they focus on activities in which they excel. The converse is also true. Most people achieve less than desired results when performing tasks that do not suit their skill sets or natural abilities. Having stated the obvious, let's evaluate all the areas of your business and clearly identify your strengths, weaknesses, and areas in need of "purposeful business improvement planning."

Dissecting your business and identifying areas of focus or improvement is a major step towards poising a business for sustainable growth. Before we can build your best brand, your best marketing practices, your best sales approaches, and biggest business, we need to build a purposeful improvement blueprint. This will serve as your guide to a new business vision that commands growth and takes marketshare as you unveil the new business offerings to the 21st century consumer base.

> ## SUCCESS STORY
>
> An entrepreneur took my course to try and figure out how to take his business to the next level. In the BHS he discovered that his biggest obstacles were customer retention and follow up (question 13 and 20). We consulted with him and implemented a customer retention program that included loyalty incentives, automation, and systematic testing of marketing solutions. As a result, his business went from 80K of gross sales in six months to 120K of gross sales in four months *at less cost to the business!* What would you do with a 225% spike in income?

Business decisions are hard enough for any business owner, but guessing what to do to be more successful is like trying to win a game of darts in the dark. You may be taking action, you may even be hitting the dartboard; but when you're guessing where to throw your business darts, the results may have you on the losing end of the business game. Honestly dissecting your business helps you to start building improvement plans with the business-lights on and illuminates your profit targets to strike the business growth bullseye.

Now, it is important to note that not every business is the

BIGGER BUSINESS BLUEPRINT

same. Different businesses have different moving parts and processes. However, it is also important to note that while a business may have different moving parts, there are some foundational aspects to every business that (for the sake of argument) remain as constants.

ORIGIN OF THE BUSINESS HONESTY SCORE

So we are about to embark on the Business Honesty Score (BHS) test. Before we get into it, let me tell you a bit about where it came from. The questions are strategic and built from the knowledge base of countless business consulting meetings, group trainings, and thousands of entrepreneurs just like you, who have businesses just like you, and the same challenges just like you. I built this *business-truth serum* Q&A test and then attached scoring values for each question to uncover the quickest business initiative path to not only your best, but also your Biggest Business Blueprint.

> Was the Business Honesty Score easy to build? No!
>
> Did marrying the right strategic business questions with the right scoring values to uncover a strategic growth path take massive trial and error? Yes!
>
> Did I shed some tears trying to perfect the scoring model? Yes!
>
> Is it worth it to help transform your business? Yes!
>
> Do you get to benefit from it as an entrepreneur that wants to grow? YES, YES, YES!

So how did I do it? Well, I've done it before. I created the same type of scoring system for a big brand in the real estate training space (where I've been speaking for roughly 15 years, training thousands in search of real estate wealth) that not only helped new investors clear the best path for investing, but actually told them which path to start investing with. It took me over 300 tests, developing the right number combinations and honing the right questions, but the end product was worth the fight. The immediate transformation was amazing.

Here is what the system did for each person that took the test. It gave them a deliberate path to get to their best investment strategy without all of the day-to-day trial and error that would break, frustrate, or sadly make most give up. With their new Personal Investment Number or P.I.N. score, they stopped wasting time on the wrong strategies and focused on the real income productive activities that produced results with precision and much welcomed clarity. A truly transformative moment.

So what does this mean for you? The same thing... a truly transformative moment. I tweaked, tested, retested, changed question structure well over 200 times, and the results are nothing short of exhilarating. Here is why: *__Your biggest foundation for a mind-numbing positive transformation to your business growth path is in the numbers__*. I've tested it countless times and the numbers don't lie! (Just as you'll see later in the marketing and sales chapter – the data and numbers don't lie!)

"BUSINESS-HONESTY-SCORE" TEST

THE #1 ENTREPRENEUR TEST FOR UNLOCKING WEALTH

Honesty is the best policy! If you want to grow faster and wake up with a real plan of attack to get there, then honestly answer the BHS test to illuminate the clearest path to your business success. The test is designed to uncover holes in your business model that are holding your company back from becoming the biggest business you can build. We cannot fix the leaks unless we can see them, and this test shines a light on the leaks in your business bucket.

I see it time and time again. Business owners are drudging along, just trying to get through the business day, and are not paying attention to some potential leaks in their business model. When you do this, in essence, you are trying to fill a leaky bucket, and when you take a free moment to look at your business, you wonder why the bucket is not full. The honest answer is there are holes in your business that you have not addressed, which has caused you to work extra hard and still not get to where you want from a goals standpoint. You have to keep working harder than you should to be profitable since the holes keep draining your income; when in reality, if you honestly address some key business items to success, and assess where the leaks are, you can start to patch the holes, fill the profit bucket easier, and give yourself more time to build the business even bigger.

So how are we going to accomplish this? By answering the following business efficiency test questions to help develop your business growth plan. Answer each question with two main criteria, *agreement measurement* and *strength measurement* for reaching your coveted Business Honesty Score. You need to assess whether or not you agree or disagree with the statement/ question, and to what degree using the scoring values 1 – 10. Additionally, you need to answer each question with a value of 1 –10 in regards to how strong or weak you (or your team) are. If you and/or your team are very weak in an area of your business, then give it a lower value, with one being the lowest value of all. If you and/or your team are very strong in an area of your business, then give it a higher value, with ten being the highest.

Special Note: If this makes you nervous, then good! It should! You are about to accomplish something 90% of business owners never accomplish!

BEFORE YOU START:

Remember: <u>Honesty</u>! This will be the *most important score you've ever received*. Imagine being given a score that transforms every business action you take moving forward. That is what your greatest attempt to honestly answer these test questions will deliver!

Score each question twice:

1. <u>Agreement Measurement 1 – 10:</u>
   A1 = **Disagree; A10 = Strongly Agree**
2. <u>Strength Level Measurement 1 – 10:</u>
   S1 = **Major Weakness; S10 = Major Strength**

BUSINESS HONESTY SCORE TEST

Q1: Are your business filings in order and are you a pro at managing the responsibilities to keep your business in good standing?

Q2: My accounting process is streamlined and I am ahead of the curve in the sharpest tax planning strategies for my industry.

Q3: I've got the right staff for my business niche and know the best places to find more when I grow.

Q4: Do I have proper insurance to protect my business well?

Q5: I have the proper compliance procedures and operating protocols in place, and they are clearly accessible for everyone to follow the same path.

Q6: My business is operating very efficiently with a _streamlined_ easy business process.

Q7: I am aware of my competition and have a good handle on where I stack up against the competition.

Q8: Consumers find it easy to do business with me in today's marketplace. In other words, there are very few hurdles to doing business and I'm very user friendly!

Q9: I know where to engage my customers best and have good brand awareness of my product in today's consumer marketplace.

Q10: I find myself working _on_ my business (High Dollar Productive Activity), rather than working _in_ my business.

Q11: I consistently seek out new ways to innovate, to run my business easier.

Q12: I feel like my business is modernized to meet the expectations of today's consumer demands for my products and services. (Innovation)

Q13: My customer relationship is at its zenith, therefore customer retention and customer profitability are right where I would like them to be.

Q14: Is my business vision crystal clear to me and all others that my business touches?

Q15: I am making the right investments in my business systematically, to not only achieve growth, but also sustain growth.

Q16: I regularly engage other business peers to help grow my business. In other words, I ask others for assessments about my business to help improve my results and offerings.

Q17: I consistently ask for feedback from co-workers and take that information to make purposeful change in a positive direction.

Q18: I track sales properly and efficiently. Others that see my sales tracking process would agree!

Q19: I track customer acquisition strategies (marketing) consistently to drill to the best sales process and maximize marketing results.

Q20: I am a leader in customer follow up. I touch my customer base often and in different ways to get more sales.

Q21: I have documented best business processes and sales efficiencies to help make my team easily produce more business.

Q22: My Unique Selling Proposition (USP) helps me stand out from the competition. I have clear separation from competitor offerings!

Q23: My offerings are very competitively priced and the value easily exceeds the expectations of every customer I touch.

Q24: If I could not work tomorrow or decided not to work for a while, would my company still thrive?

Q25: I consistently test my marketing online and offline in different manners to maximize business sales and data driven knowledge.

After completing the questionnaire, circle the top ten questions that provided the lowest numbered responses. These are most likely the areas of your business that need the most attention for sustainability and growth. An On-Purpose CEO will take their Business Honesty Score and use this as their guide to immediately address what business items need the most attention. This will start to reveal your fastest blueprint to growth and an even more exciting blueprint to fast-tracking wealth!

UNLOCKING YOUR BHS SCORE: LEVERAGING KNOWLEDGE TO SMART BUSINESS DECISIONS

1. **Building Your Growth Path:** Add up the scores to each question for positioning. It is creating your *Best Business Growth Prioritization Path*. You can now breakdown tasks starting with the lowest total score first and ascend to the higher scores, for a clear and purposeful business growth to-do list. (I typically tell my consulting clients to address the top ten first, but some create action items for all 25.)

2. **Priorities:** When using the scoring system model to develop your business growth prioritization path, *consider ranking the items with a low strength score as a higher priority,* because it is addressing your business from an area of weakness.

3. **BHS Scoring Buckets:** (Max Score = 500) The different B.H.S Scoring Buckets tell you what type of help you may want to seek first to fast track your business growth.

    A. 425 – 500 (B.S. – Go retake the test! You were not honest enough!)

    B. 350 – 424 (Process and Growth Refinement)

C. 250 – 349 (Business Building and Process Development)

D. 100 – 249 (Business Structure Construction and Development)

E. 0 – 99   (Get a Job or Skip to Chapter on Leverage ASAP)

SPECIAL NOTE:

Any questions with individual scores less than a total of five need immediate attention and weekly updated actionable commitment until you feel it is back above a minimum combined score of 12. From experience, you have to fill that gap before it gets wider and slows growth.

CEO RESOURCE: If you want specific business resources and action item suggestions for specific test questions, go to www.BHShelp.com for the blueprint.

In later chapters we will dive into how to use the honest answers to build your best, purpose-driven business. For now, we just need to get down to the business nitty-gritty and identify some clear areas for improvement.

TIME MANAGEMENT

It is very difficult for most business owners to improve and get clear with their business initiatives when they get dragged into the "what is on fire first syndrome," that seemingly sucks the life out of almost each business day. With the advent of technology today, it is easy to see why this can happen. We are all so connected with technology, that the e-mail you checked first thing this morning (probably from your phone and you checked it from bed), may now be the driving force on how your day starts. This can drain the productivity out of even the most focused business owner.

This *Business Honesty Score* helps cut through the business clutter and definitively shows you what your major focus should be. At first glance, you may be thinking: Where do I start and how am I going to tackle all of this? The B.H.S. shows you where to start, so that is solved. The answer to the question, "How am I going to tackle all of this?" is simple. You will tackle it just like you would tackle eating an elephant, which is one bite at a time.

What this business expansion test is designed to do, is to help you identify where to devote real business problem-solving efforts as a precursor to implementing real positive business transformation initiatives. In essence, helping you step closer and closer to CEO business gold, which is clearing the problem areas away purposefully and systematically, so you can focus on *High Dollar Productive Activities* that grow the business.

It is nearly impossible to focus on High Dollar Productive Activities when other areas of your business need attention which have not been addressed. The mark of an On-Purpose CEO is one who identifies areas where improvement is needed, addresses the areas with possible solutions, tracks the potential solutions progressively, and documents permanent, tested solutions. If you practice this on-purpose business growth process in the areas where you need to improve, then you can implement and solve all the way to the Bigger Business Blueprint finish line, which is where you ultimately win the business profitability and sustainability battle.

The ultimate prize with this business practice exercise is to identify and tackle the apparent challenges with progress towards solutions, which frees you up to focus on High Dollar Productive Activities (HDPA). The more we can keep you living in the HDPA space, where you are serving the company best by creating larger income opportunities, the more growth your company can experience on-purpose.

The bottom line is that *you cannot buy more time*, you can only look to solve time problems with purposeful solutions, tracking to eliminate wasted business time, in order to focus more time on HDPA or the money makers for your business.

You'll see later in the chapter called "Leverage" that solutions to help your business grow can be achieved in a few different ways. The key is to explore the options to leverage you and your business effectively, and give you and your sales team the freedom to grow the business. By addressing the deficiencies revealed in your BHS test, you gain leverage to tackle the big revenue generators because the other areas of your business are running smoother.

POST BUSINESS HONESTY SCORE TEST ACTIVITY:

- Take the scores from your BHS Test and write down your top potential actions for each section to increase your business productivity, any resources to help, and assign the right person for the job. (If you are a one-man/woman-band then most activities will be on you, unless you apply leverage to the business equation, as you'll see in chapter eight.)

- Rank them in order of importance to develop a better and clearer path to a bigger business.

- How much time do you think you should devote to solving your business inefficiency? In your opinion, of course, add a real time value to complete each.

- Prepare to discuss some of the solutions and business initiatives with your team ASAP! (Sharing the vision helps move the herd in one direction!)

Spend time reviewing the questions you answered and develop what you think might be potential actions to reach solutions for each. Congrats, because now you are really starting to *"Get Intimate"* with your business by breaking down your business into smaller achievable actions, to fine-tune the separate moving parts on a much more intimate, purposeful, and meaningful level. This separation is where you, as the On-Purpose CEO, can see a much clearer path to business building growth, versus the old By-Accident CEO that lets that day's fire dictate their business focus. Knowing your business on this deeper level gives you the competitive edge you deserve to tackle initiatives more clearly, and more easily, to put more income in your pocket.

It should also be noted that these questions are simply a guideline to help zero-in on areas for business improvement. The goal for the test is to uncover some business improvement items to be addressed systematically. Now, whether your specific business hurdles were addressed or not, these questions are vital to every successful business. By all means, attach these to your specific needs as enhancement criteria to putting your biggest and best business-foot forward.

> **CEO TIP:** Track your time spent each day running the business. When you know where your time is spent, efficiency plans evolve!

> **CEO RESOURCE:** To track time, you might try www.timedoctor.com

Chapter 2:

Developing The Best Business Process

Developing the best business process starts with asking a few important questions. Is my sales process from lead to customer easy, or not? Can anyone close business with my current process? How long will it take to train someone to master my process to close meaningful business? Is my process the most efficient it can be for today's standards?

There is no doubt that the process to close business is important for any CEO, but to take a giant step towards becoming an *On-Purpose Business*, the better question to answer is, "How can I make the process even better?" One bone crushing way to get more sales and/or larger profits is to make the process simpler. This can be done by eliminating steps to close, or what I call unnecessary time wasters, and by automating some of the process. The faster we can help you simplify the sales process, the faster we can help you to get to retirement.

The bottom line is that we live in a convenience world today, where consumers will sacrifice quality for the ease of doing business. Make it easier for a prospect to become your customer, because your business vitality depends on it. So, our next business move is to map out your sales process and then look for ways to simplify the process.

GIVE OTHERS THE BLUEPRINT...

One great thing about blueprinting and sharing your best process (or step-by-step sales funnel) is that it can identify if "your way" is one of the logjams that keeps the business from growing. This is a polite way of saying that you cannot be the one that stands in the way of growth because you are not willing to take steps towards process improvement. You can't be the only one that knows the process or the business cannot grow without you. You have to give others the blueprint for business leverage. If you want to create a business that has a chance for you to leave a legacy for generations to come, then you must clearly define your process and at some point in the future train your replacement. Otherwise, you will always be working "In" your business and not truly "On" your business. Even worse, the business will always be dependent on you to grow, which is not the best sustainable business model.

It should be a standard business practice to consistently devote time to improving your business process, and constantly be seeking to gain more knowledge to improve. "Everyone in business and everything in business can become obsolete, so you better _learn for your life!_" Constantly look to improve. Constantly seek to learn (invest in yourself) to help you and your business processes evolve.

> **CEO Tip:** "Winning CEOs always look to refine their process. It makes cents!" –Jason Palliser

Whether your process is easier than most, or harder than most, is irrelevant. Not defining the best sales process you can, and then sharing the process, is an *On-Accident* CEO mistake. Here is why. In the event that "YOU" are not available to make sure things are moving along correctly, there isn't anyone to man the *Business Process Ship*. Not only is mapping out the process to simplify a smart business decision, it is a vital part of your business's future survival. Map out your current process in a document and put real brainpower towards improving it.

Once you've built out your process, as an *On-Purpose* CEO, you should ask for help! Ask others what they think, ask employees what they think, or even better, ask your current customers how you could improve the process. Trust me, your current customers know how your process could improve and they are not afraid to tell you. Listen, refine and improve. Remember to get the process on paper (or digital paper – word doc) so the best plans are out of your head. He or she, whom documents best, wins! You win because when things are mapped out or in writing, they can be shared! If everything is in your head, then you are the logjam. Define a better, more efficient process and then get out of your own way... all the way to the bank.

> **CEO Non-Negotiable:** Always Seek To Improve The Process!

CEO Resource: Get a jumpstart on the process documenting by downloading your complimentary worksheet at:
BiggerBusinessBlueprint.com/ProcessMap

DEFINING YOUR SALES PROCESS...

Spend time thinking about every part of the process to close business. You could get as granular as, "What time you need to start the daily process," if you know it increases your chances for sales. Here is the time to be very deliberate, since this will come to serve as your roadmap for others to follow your clear business vision in the future.

I would like to make a strong business suggestion to help your process get better. After you are done with this book, I would like you to share your process with someone that is outside of your arena, and ask him or her to critique it. Why? Because the feedback you get from them may unlock bags of cash from your process-vault that you did not see before because you were too close to the process to see an easier solution to sales. Another reason for this is to see if they can even follow your sales process. If they cannot, then you most certainly want to find the areas where the process may be unclear and strive to simplify even deeper to help future business growth.

Again, the truth will set you free. Just because "you know your process," does not mean that the rest of the universe can easily follow your process blueprint to wealth. One big key to a more valuable business is to build it to run on its own. Why? Because people and companies can get behind what they clearly understand. People cannot get behind what they do not understand with any level of confidence, which in-turn hurts the value and survivability of your business. Build your best, clear and deliberate process to closing business, as well as retaining future business. Constantly refine it like your business life depends on it - because it does. *The better the process, the better the business!*

MIND MAPPING

Each business is different, but no matter what business you have, there is always a process to closing the sale, and there are always moving parts. It is time to start mapping out those moving parts to look for ways to improve the process. Getting very clear with your business process can unlock massive income potential. The more detailed you can be with your entire process (start-to-finish), the more clear it may become for you and others to see how your business cycle works and help it improve.

SUCCESS STORY

MIND MAPPING SHALL SET YOU FREE

A few years ago a consulting client needed help moving his business forward. One of the main struggles was freeing up his time to do business growth activities. We created a mindmap of all the things that he did on a weekly basis. What we discovered was that on any given day, he had his hands in every aspect of his business. He was at a complete **logjam.**

We identified the top two to three things he actually HAD to do and then put together a plan to offload the rest of the responsibilities. Over the next month he documented how he wanted everything done, created videos, and screen-captured processes.

Once he was able to offload the minutiae of his day-to-day business to a virtual assistant, he was free to pursue the truly *High Dollar Productive Activities* that would grow his business. Success!

I strongly suggest you use mapping software to build out your process. I recommend either www.Mindjet.com (a cost) or www.xmind.net (free). There are two big reasons for this. The first reason is that great plans locked away in your CEO head, inhibit growth potential. For you to grow and become bigger, you cannot be the logjam in your business. Having a map that can be easily updated and shared, helps to ensure that your master plans are not hidden away inside your CEO brain where they cannot be shared. For example, you may have a good process and it may be clear to you; but if it is all in your head, then you might as well burn thousands of income dollars. You are going to be wasting hours and hours of valuable *High Dollar Productive Activity* time trying to get others to see your vision and process. Mapping software can help you get out of your own way to let the business grow.

Secondly, if you map it out once in a mind map, you can TWEAK and CHANGE it easily, forever. Then your process becomes nimble, allowing for changes on the fly. Mapping out your process can make you millions. It is the fastest way I have come across to get ideas, thoughts, and business process out of your head and organized fast.

MIND MAPPING AWESOMENESS

Mapping your ideas and business process has become so easy with software like I mentioned previously, that I can talk to any consulting client and in less than 20 minutes I can have a map in front of their eyes to clearly show them process, business flow, and growth opportunities that normal conversation could never flush out. My favorite aspect of mind mapping your best business, is that it gets all of the clutter out of your head (fast) on a topic, and then allows you to "drag and drop" any item on the map to a new spot to organize the scattered thoughts lightning fast.

Here are some core business process items to consider when building your best business growth process. Build a map around each of these separate processes. You can combine them later, if you want, for a bone-crushing business flow machine that others can see, digest, and get behind.

CEO CHALLENGE:

I challenge you to stop reading right now for 60 seconds and pull up your calendar and schedule a 30-minute appointment for tomorrow that says, "download free mind mapping software and create a new map." You want to change your business life forever? Then do it now. Next, set a 20-minute timer and create a new map and label the topic "My Perfect Work Day." Click to insert 10 sub-topics and insert items that would deliver your perfect workday. Do it fast! Add items in any order.

After you've spilled your business-guts into the map, then click the mouse and drag them into your perfect order! If you want to go deeper, then right-click on the subtopics and add another subtopic for that item. List the best approach, resource, and/or best practice to crush that item. Do it for each and now you have a clear map to your best day. Save it and then once a month, come back to it for review, to add to it, or tweak, to constantly improve your best business day.

This is a home run for my consulting clients. Every time they leave our initial two-hour business consulting meeting, they have a map that turns them into a monster. I cannot even explain how powerful it is for them to see their business broken down into a concise and digestible map. After seeing the map, my consulting clients can usually tell me where the problem is, which more often than not, is different from the initial conversation because they can now see everything out of their head on a business map. I love this process. Send me your "Perfect Business Work Day" at *Jason@goseejason.com* so I can see it. I always love seeing results and I may even sprinkle some free advice on your map. (Time permitting of course.)

The Sales Process Moving Parts:

- Cold Calls
- Follow up
- Signing Documents
- Updating Offers / Sales Postings
- Client Management
- Placing Orders / Tracking Shipments
- Client Survey
- Website Management
- Accounting Measures
- Marketing Placement

Set a timer for 20 minutes and create a new mind map for each topic. See how much you can spill out of your CEO brain about the topic, fast. Take a break and repeat the process for each. Then I would right-click each leg and add a sub-topic that attaches some sort of potential improvement or leverage to that item if you can. Now you are marching forward with an on-purpose business approach.

When processes are spelled out to the Nth degree, it is easy to take your process and look to refine and simplify. Also, when you get very granular it is much easier to drill down to the best business process because you can separate the moving parts to individually divide and conquer if needed. Once you feel as if you are done, take five minutes to see if you can add even more legs to your map and take your process even deeper. The deeper, the better! When you really try to drill deeper than you think is possible, what can come out of your efforts is new insight to process improvement, and clearer vision on where resources may be needed.

CEO Resource: Mind Mapping Software
www.xmind.net Or *www.mindjet.com*

CEO Resource: Check out this video to see Mind Maps in Action:

BiggerBusinessBlueprint.com/MindMapTutorial

Review it often for improvement. If you show me a business owner that reviews their process often to improve, then I'll show you a business owner that is working "On" their business and making more money, as opposed to a business owner that is working "In" their business. And lastly, I'd be willing to bet that you are looking at a business CEO that has experienced sales growth and achieved it much easier. *Get clear with your business and achieve growth.*

PROCESS SIMPLIFICATION

Now that you have a process map in front of you, do everything within your power to "*SIMPLIFY*" the process. Simplification can deliver more profitability and produce increased sales with less effort. Make it a non-negotiable standard business practice to find easier processes to achieve growth. In fact, you cannot afford not to make it your monthly mission. Today's customers want things fast, easy, and right now. A sure fire way to lose marketshare and profitability is to have a less than stellar customer sales process. As the old adage goes, "Good news travels fast, but bad news travels even faster." A less than exceptional process can be the catalyst that causes you to play constant business catch up, by working way too hard to keep clients and employees happy. Simplify all the way to the business bank!

Here are some items that I address with business owners when teaching or consulting to help simplify their business and spark deeper business thought...

Simplification and Streamlining Examples:

- Live sales team vs. message callbacks (Speed Closes!)
- Going paperless - Resource: www.hellosign.com
- Automate Your Lead Responses – Fast E-mails
- "Buy Data" instead of "Mining" for it.
  Resource: www.listsource.com
- Automate Payroll – Eliminates Several Steps
- Template Everything! Auto-Fill Forms
- Eliminate Back and Forth For Appointments:
  Cloud Calendar! www.youcanbookme.com (Google Integration)

CEO TIP: An On-Purpose CEO (which you are) would also put another independent set of eyes on it to seek their feedback. They may see something obvious to an outsider that you couldn't see (because you are too close to the process). Their input may bring to light an even smarter operational efficiency to land you even more business. All you have to do is simply make plans to revisit your process often. Not too hard, huh?

CEO RESOURCE:

Targeted Lists and Data:
www.listability.com, www.listsource.com, and *www.melissadata.com*

Paperless Document Signing: *www.hellosign.com*

Online Appointment Setting: *youcanbookme.com*

STAY UP TO DATE!

Marketplace evolution is the destroyer of the perfect process, so plan for it! The marketplace is an ever-changing landscape that may command your business to adapt or lose business. Knowing this fact should hopefully adjust your business mindset to adopt a better business-building philosophy that centers on systematic process refinement. Systematically seek the "pursuit of process perfection" on a consistent basis. The moment you rest, the competition is gaining, so strategically seek to keep raising the business-process bar, and leave the competition grasping at straws while your profits spike.

My suggestion is to visit the process map every month to see if there is any room for improvement. With a detailed map already in place, it makes monthly refinement exploration very easy.

BUSINESS BACKBONE

The final step to getting intimate with your business is to know your business body inside out! *So our last stop is to focus on our business backbone.* It addresses all of the important parts of your business that keep everything together.

I think it is fair to say that when looking at the body, the backbone is not the sexiest part, but most people would agree that it is a critical part of the body to hold everything together. Your business is no different.

Items such as business tax filings and company certifications/compliance are vital to the health of your business. So here are some things to think about with each requirement to keep your business healthy, hopefully wealthy, and strong.

Your business filings are necessary to make sure your company is in good standing with local, state, and other various agencies. If you dread the thought of keeping these filings up to date, then ask your bookkeeper and/or CPA to handle it for you. Forgetting a filing can be costly and we are trying to run a profitable business "On Purpose," so take the burden off of you to keep you working on the business. If you are having a CPA run the books for you, you may want to consider a bookkeeper as a buffer between you and the CPA, which can save you on bottom line costs and increase your cash flow. (Hint: Hire a Virtual Bookkeeper.)

As far as business bank accounts and business insurance goes, do not just settle with what you already know because it is comfortable. I always teach business owners that I consult with, "*In order to retire comfortable, sometimes you need to do the uncomfortable!*" Here is what I mean: It is your job as the On-Purpose CEO to make sure that you are getting the very best for your company. You should talk to no less than five banks and five insurance companies to get quotes on costs and benefits before bringing your business to them. They have competition just like you, so they should have to earn your business, just like you have to earn business from the marketplace.

Again, we are dissecting your business from the inside out and striking a new banking relationship can save you tons of money, as well as finding the right insurance company to insure your business. As an example, I have insurance on one of my business ventures and the cost was roughly $2,400 per year. I systematically check for better rates every year and found the same coverage for roughly $1,050 per year. Isn't that smart business?

CEO Tip: Simple... Simple... Simple - Increase Profitability Without Making A Sale

I gave my business an income boost by simply making it a non-negotiable to check for rates regularly. If fact, think about this; you would have to give the same information to each place to quote you services. So, once you have it organized, simply forward the same package to a few different places to see what they can do for you.

SIMPLIFICATION TIP: Turn your "Vacation Reminder" on and build a sales e-mail that will always reply back with your best message so you look like a follow up freak of nature. "Doesn't have to be used for just vacation, it can help you take more vacations!"

> **CEO NON-NEGOTIABLE:** Always get quotes from five places before making your business decisions.

CASH FLOW

Sales and positive cash flow are what keep the business going. Without either, the business will not survive. If you are not already, you need to make sure that you have very detailed tracking data for cash flow. You can have lots of sales, but if you do not have a real handle on the business cash flow, the results can be less than favorable. If you have not done so already, build a steel trap around your cash flow process to make it easy for you and others to have real time access to where the monthly cash flow sits. This knowledge is necessary in order to make and implement intelligent business building decisions.

We will be diving into ways to increase sales and cash flow in future chapters. For now we just need to make sure that you are really focused on collecting and tracking the data. Tracking

Chapter 3:

Building A Brand That Lasts!

"TIME TO STOP WINKING IN THE DARK!"

If it is the truth, then we need to face it. There are tons of great people in the world. There are tons of great ideas in the world. There are tons of great products in the world... *but not great Brands*!

There are not tons of great brands in the world! In fact, most entrepreneurs are guilty of this business tragedy. They have great ideas, they even create and have great products, but they are lacking any sort of brand identity, which can be the death of a business. In today's sharing society, lack of brand identity can kill your business. If fact, if you anchor in and really focus on building a strong brand and brand identity, then you can experience massive growth and have the rest of the universe do it for you.

Why is your brand so important? Because a good brand can bring in easy sales. Because it can cement your business in the minds of your best targeted consumers. Because a good brand can take on a life of its own. Because it can increase the sale price of your products when your brand is positioned well.

A good brand and good brand positioning can set your business on fire! Good branding can set the stage for the world to go crazy with your brand. Your strong branding efforts can add "zeros" to your bank account like wildfire. Commanding attention and exploding your digital business footprint is what GOOD BRANDING today is all about (Awareness, Increased Exposure, and Increased Sales).

I've seen it countless times. Good idea, great product, and no branding, which equals empty bank accounts in today's competitive marketplace. It is sad to say, but most business owners' products are essentially "the world's best kept secret." They are winking in the dark with their product offerings due to a lack of real branding. In this chapter we will look to lay the foundation for building a brand poised, not only to be a player in the marketplace, but also to dominate it.

BRANDING FOOD FOR THOUGHT...

"If you don't manage your brand, someone will do it for you, and that somebody will likely be your competitor." - Donald Trump

Some business owners have made the CEO decision to put their head in the business sand and say, "I'm doing it the way I've always done it," and let the fast moving marketplace pass them by. They have failed to purposefully unveiled their brand to the world today. They are in the dark ages and would rather build an underground bunker than a brand that can be consumed online 24 hours a day. They take the attitude of "no one will find me online and learn more about my business" (conspiracy theorists is what I call them). They take the stance that they don't want their information on the Internet because they don't trust it. Well, that is perfect because if you are my competitor, then you are the easiest brand to destroy. In reality, if they embraced commerce the way it organically lives today, they would experience growth like they have never seen before.

If you are trying to combat the undeniable staple of the online universe as a business foundation for your brand awareness, then I can say with confidence that you may be fighting an uphill battle. Why? With the Internet revolution here to stay, if you are my competitor and you are hiding (not digitizing your brand), then I can simply just post a couple of negative comments online about your business. That is all anyone will find when they search for your company (and they will search my conspiracy theory business friends), and I will take your customers. You don't want that, right?

So what do we do? We anchor in and look to take complete control of our brand. We let the world know what we want them to know about our brand, instead of our competitors. The larger we grow your digital brand reach, the easier it is to grab new customers and push any negative information down the online search engine charts.

> <u>Brand Fact:</u> Negative information will reach your company. It is not a question of "if," it is a question of "when" it will happen. You can't please everyone every time! In fact, I always tell clients, "If you have not had any detractors to your business yet, then you're simply not popular enough yet!" – Jason Palliser

Here is a good explanation of why you need to be in control of your brand and your digital footprint from an expert on the subject:

There's a serious disconnect between business owners and consumers.

What people say about your company online has become the single most important reflection of your company's quality, reliability, and skill. It doesn't matter if you're a dentist, a plastic surgeon, a carpet cleaner, or a painter. In a 2015 local consumer review survey, **92% of global consumers indicated they trust online reviews** from strangers when making purchasing decisions.

When review sites like "Yelp" started to surface on the web, many companies failed to assess the impact they would eventually have on their ability to generate new leads and new customers. Companies with positive reviews **can convert 183% more new business** than a business with negative or no reviews.

Most business owners don't realize **75% of people** don't believe that companies tell the truth in advertisements. Advertising allows you to pat yourself on the back and tell everyone how great you are. But the fact is that consumers trust what other people say about your business more than they trust what you say about your business.

Despite these statistics and the obvious buying habits and decisions made by consumers, many small business owners still do not recognize the importance of online reviews and their reputations.

In fact, a lot of businesses avoid the topic altogether as if they're hoping it will just go away... but that's very unlikely. So instead of ignoring reviews, it's time to embrace and leverage them for success.

To make sure the world knows what we want them to know about your business, we are going to systematically grow your digital footprint, so that when consumers search, they learn what we want them to learn about you (versus the what the competitor might want them to think).

BRANDING EXCELLENCE PRINCIPLES:

"Your business without advertising is like winking at a girl in the dark! You know what your are doing, but nobody else does!" -Stuart Henderson

My favorite marketing and branding quote of all time is from Stuart Henderson. In fact, I would expand it to say, "Your business without proper branding and marketing is like winking at a girl in the dark. You know what you're doing, but nobody else does!" I sincerely hope that stings your CEO ego a little bit. No more winking in the dark!

With this in mind, we are going to explore the following branding principles to purposefully build your business:

- Know Your Competition
- U.S.P. – Unique Selling Proposition!
- Naming Your Company or Brand
- Your Tagline
- Positioning – What to cement in consumers' minds?

- Your Story– Will consumers feel your story?
- Brand Tangibles – Logo, Website, Brochures, Tag Line!
- Consistency Wins! – Easy, Catchy, Memorable

KNOW YOUR COMPETITION!

Not knowing what your competition is doing is like trying to win a game of hide and seek with a ghost! You are never going to win. I see so many business owners take action with a good idea, only to sputter out because they've thrown a brand together without any direction or real purpose. We first have to see what others are doing to scout out a safe place to land on the branding battlefield.

As an On-Purpose CEO to your business, I would block out an entire day and sit down to research everything you can on your product niche. See what pops up when you search online (the 21st century way of doing things, of course), and then compile a list of competitors. Spend time diving into their product offering, their website, their promotions, their pricing, and get to know them well. To beat your opponent, you need to know your opponent.

After finding your competitors, I would narrow your focus down to the top three to five, and focus even deeper on them. The best thing you can do to build a better brand is scout the competition. I suggest taking it to the highest level you can, and become a client (if you can) to secret shop them. Why, you might ask? Because if you have gone through their entire process, then you can make informed decisions on how to offer a better product. As an example, wouldn't it be good to know that when you buy their product or service, that the experience gets derailed when it comes to customer follow up? Of course it would.

After you've done everything you can to know everything about your competition, then it is time to ask yourself the sharpest branding question your can to be a better brand: "How are we better?" When you can definitively answer that question, then you have a rock solid foundation from which to build your winning brand!

> **CEO Non-Negotiable:** Always Scout The Competition!

CEO Resource: Scout the competition video: BiggerBusinessBlueprint.com/ScoutTips

CEO Resource: *www.whatrunswhere.com* - Tells you where your competitors place their ads and which ones get the best results! Take their millions in trial and error and compete with them in the same arenas for a fraction of the costs! I call that a CEO Checkmate!

UNIQUE SELLING PROPOSITION

A *Unique Selling Proposition* is something that separates your product offering from the rest of the competition. In other words, it is the item or items that make you different from the rest of your free-market competition. I tell business owners all of the time, not to confuse Unique Selling Proposition with Best Selling Proposition. What I mean is simply this: "You don't have to be the best in a group of others striving to be the best, you simply just need to be different!" Your "different" needs to be compelling enough to make someone switch to your brand or choose your brand, and then you are well on your way - marching towards the best brand you can be.

> **Unique Selling Proposition Example: TOMS Shoes**
>
> A good example of having one of the best USP, but not the best product, is TOMS Shoes. They do not claim to be the BEST so you must buy their shoes. They simply claim to make real comfortable shoes and their USP (or their big differentiator) is that when you buy their product you are helping a deserving kid also get a pair of shoes! How is that for standing out from the crowd? Imagine the feeling most people get when they buy a pair of "TOMS." They not only walk out with a good pair of comfortable shoes, they can also hold their head high for the rest of the day knowing that they are supporting those in need. I don't know about you, but for me that is branding genius.

Consider the TOMS Shoes example when you are coming up with your USP. "How can I be different?" is a much better question to answer than, "How can I be the best?" After all, showing how you are different can be apparent and much easier than showing you're the best. "The best" is always up for interpretation and argument, whereas being different (if done well) is rarely up for debate.

> **CEO RESOURCE:** Having trouble with a USP? Make an appointment to discuss it with me here: BiggerBusinessBlueprint.com/USPHelp

NAMING YOUR COMPANY/BRAND

When coming up with your brand name and tag line, do your best to keep it easy, catchy, and memorable. You probably have a company name already and that is fine, as you'll see in the next paragraph. All I'm saying is at least do your business the favor of giving your brand the best chance to become an industry staple in your niche. In other words, don't make the naming so unique that it is hard to remember, let alone spell. You're creating your own hurdles to doing business if your brand is a mouthful. I always preach, "The simpler the better," when it comes to strategically naming your brand.

You may have already named your company. That is fine. You may have noticed I said, "naming your brand," and not naming your company. Here is why: I know that this chapter may be a source of pain for you, because after learning some branding non-negotiables you may be rethinking your company name. Let me slow down and help you out a little bit here. I did not say that you had to re-name your company if you know it needs some branding help (which most businesses do). Having said that, there is nothing stopping you from keeping the same business name and coming up with a better "Brand Name" and tag line to build your brand legacy around. In fact, I've done this a few times where I have "paperwork" that states my company name, yet I use a D.B.A. document or Doing-Business-As document to build my company around my selected brand name and tag line.

What does that mean for you? It simply means that you can have your company bank accounts, filings, insurance and more in the company name, while using a D.B.A. to identify with the rest of the outside world. Example: I had a company that was named R.E.I. XXX for tax purposes, but the brand name using my D.B.A. was something different. (i.e. REI BlackBook for real estate automation.)

The reason I have mentioned this here is simple. The more catchy, easy, and memorable you can make your public brand in the consumer's eyes, the easier you can grow as a 21st century business. If you think you need to re-brand, then explore it. Your business, pocketbook, and brand advocates deserve it.

If you are not sure, then ask others their opinion. (Warning: whatever they say is right because they are the customers!)

> ## SUCCESS STORY
>
> I consulted for an employer benefits company that was winning with unions, but failing to gain marketshare with non-union business. Their company name and brand said "union" to prospective non-union clients. The feedback they were getting was, "We want to try your service, but management is afraid you are going to try to organize and unionize our employees."
>
> Through my consulting services we identified the issues with the brand, as well as concerns in the marketplace surrounding employee benefits. Many prospective clients were concerned by lack of transparency and horror stories of employee benefit service companies gone wrong. To address these issues, we rebranded the company, and added a tagline that included "total" and "trusted." The result was more non-union business opportunity success!

If you are too attached to your company name and do not want to change it (and I'm not saying you need to at all), then try to come up with a great business tag line that brings "it" (it – being brand awareness) all together. Remember, you are the CEO and if you need to tweak that business brand, then do it instead of standing in the way of growth and prosperity.

If you need some creative help because creativity is not your strong suit, then this next resource may be perfect for you. A very good resource to help you pick your brand name and/or tag line is www.namingforce.com, which has tons of creative minds waiting to win your money.

The people at namingforce.com will read your short story of what you are looking for and then flip the creative switch and start posting tons of suggestions for you to choose from. The way it works is that you pledge a certain amount of money to the best entry that helps you build your company brand. There will be a contest period with tons of suggestions based upon your company contest story and a voting period to see what suggestions start to rise to the top. The way someone wins the money you pledged is when the voting period has ended, you choose the one you like best and they win the money. Seriously check it out. Tons of creative people helping you collectively brainstorm on some sexy names and tag lines for your company is pretty ingenious. I wish I had thought of this concept. Use it to your advantage.

CEO Resource: *www.namingforce.com*

YOUR "TAG LINE"

If used properly, a company tag line can take on a life of its own. It can be the homing beacon for your brand. Strategically it can serve as a brand anchor for your product or service. The best tag lines keep your brand constantly in the consumer's mind or what marketing peeps call having, "Top-Of-Mind-Awareness." Hitting a business home run with your tag line can exude branding gold because it is *soooo* catchy that it is almost harder to forget than to remember. That is when you know you've hit tag line gold! Essentially, your strategic tag line is circling the wagons around your brand name to cement your position in the marketplace.

Good Tag Line Example: Nike "Just Do It."

The simpler you can make your tag line, the better. Also keep in mind that sometimes your tag may need to be more descriptive since you may be new to the marketplace and you don't have the luxury of having a mega simple tag line. Once you have cemented yourself in the marketplace, you can always go back and simplify your tag even more. Don't be scared to tweak over time. The world is not static and your brand shouldn't be either.

BRAND POSITIONING – "FIND YOUR POSITION AND BUILD A FORTRESS AROUND IT!"

Brand positioning sounds similar to USP, but it is actually the next step in your brand's evolution. It has more to do with trying to occupy and own a part of your current and future customer's brain, rather than showing why you are different. The difference here is that you want to own a feeling in the consumer's mind that your USP embodies. The aforementioned example was Toms Shoes where they donate shoes. That is the USP, but the brand positioning they are looking to own is the part of the consumer's mind that is centered on feeling helpful, philanthropic, giving, and so on. You get it? They want to own a space that no other shoe company owns, which is "buy from us and you are doing good by the world" and no other shoe company does "THAT" better! They win!

So for your company, seek tirelessly to take your USP and build around that one feeling that you want to own in your consumer's mind. Build your brand and marketing around cementing that feeling in your customer every branding and marketing chance you get.

YOUR STORY...

Another brand building non-negotiable is weaving your "story" into your brand. Your story is important to your overall brand because as you strive to create a loyal following, people want to get to know the "Why?" your company does what it does, along with getting to know the person behind the curtain, depending on your type of business. This is important because for some consumers, making the decision to buy from you hinges on whether or not they feel good about you. You and your company story must earn the consumer's trust and hard-earned cash when making their final buying decision.

A simpler way to put this is that people do business with people and companies they feel like they know and like. Remember what I said earlier (for you conspiracy theorists trying to hide from the 21st century), if you've been trying to hide from the information and technology highway, then how can consumers make the decision to invest in you when they don't know you exist? Plus, if you are hard to find today and your competition decides to pick on you online, then when people do search for you, all they might find is strategic less-than-favorable reviews that may or may not be true! But at that point, it probably doesn't matter because the damage has already been done. Don't make it hard for consumers to get onboard with your brand. Make it easier by getting your brand and branding-why message out there for consumption like an On-Purpose CEO.

How do you do this? Well, as part of building your best brand, you need to tell consumers the "Why" you are here in the marketplace, and "Why" you are here to serve their needs. Come up with your best reasons why and build that into your "About Us" section on your website. Build it into a welcome video that you can shoot from your smart phone and upload to your YouTube channel for the world to see. The best part of all is that you are getting to convey what you want about you and your company brand, as opposed to your competition dictating it to your consumers. Remember, I said that we are going to take control of your brand versus your competition. Well here is just one more giant branding step towards showcasing your brand for the world to see and digest 24/7 - because that is what they demand today.

CEO Non-Negotiable: Start a YouTube channel – Create a welcome video and convey your story.

BRAND TANGIBLES

When putting the final touches on your brand creation or brand transformation, you need to devote energy to making sure you get a tangible brand facelift, if needed. Remember, this is part of that "winking in the dark" we touched upon. Don't put all of this work you've created back in the closet by not making sure that your tangible public brand is visible to the outside consumer world. It may seem childish, but if you did that, then I may have to hunt you down to stick you in the Irresponsible CEO corner for a business time out - and no one wants that.

So to avoid a CEO Time-Out, you need to make sure that your USP, your story, your positioning and everything else associated with your brand, make it to the right places for public consumption. Make sure your website conveys your branding message. Get a welcome video on your YouTube channel and share it with your website and other social medias. Make your company and brand easy to digest through a user friendly and mobile friendly website. Make sure your logo fits all different types of media so it does not look distorted. Other items to keep consistent are your e-mail signatures, brochures, and event collateral.

BRAND TANGIBLES CHECKLIST:

- Website – The corporate story on your site? The USP? Is it mobile friendly? User friendly?

- Logo – What colors? How does it appear on other medias as a discussion item?
- Tag Line – Strategically display a simple mental hook that keeps "top-of-mind-awareness" at its zenith.
- Brochures and Event Collateral should display website, logo, and tag line.
- E-mail Signatures – Logos, tag lines, and purchase links

CONSISTENCY ALWAYS WINS!

The key to building a loyal following with your brand is *being consistent*! Consistency is also the hardest branding non-negotiable component to keep on track. The cold hard business fact is that most company owners do not place too much importance on their branding initiatives until another brand comes along and starts to eat away at their marketshare and profitability. That is a shame because a brand, when well executed, can keep producing waves of new customers while those same *consistent branding* waves keep pushing their competition further and further out to sea.

Not paying attention to your brand and branding can sink your business income. *To avoid this business branding quicksand you need to become a branding consistency monster* with your marketing! How? By consistently attacking your marketplace (online and offline) with your branding message. Yes, it is that simple. Keep pumping the message out. Do it with purpose and not desperation. He or she whom is always out there in front of current and potential customers, with good branding and content, will win the marketshare battle.

Brand Building is not a part time job! Today's winning brands never sleep! Your brand is not part time, so never take time off from branding yourself and your company offerings. The competition is waiting for you to take a branding breather. Living in the age of instant information through technology, a brand cannot afford to take a business-breather.

The other part of brand consistency you want to make sure you master is maintaining a consistent message. In other words, make sure any and all of your branding and marketing materials lead the consumer market back to your same USP and company positioning. Sometimes, in an effort to try to stay in the public eye, business owners will send out content that is off the company beaten path, just to see what they get. More often than not, what they find is that they have confused their consumer base with a mixed marketing message and as the old saying goes, "The confused mind doesn't buy!"

So the name of the branding game here is to lead all branding material down the same company mantra path. Equally as important, is to make sure that you consistently or regularly have the brand message out the door to procure customers, as well as create brand loyalty. In essence, consistency can kill your competition. A tip to keep the brand alive and well is to either hire a virtual assistant (which we will talk about later) to schedule marketing regularly or use a scheduling tool to help you with your online marketing. A good example of a tool to help schedule your social media marketing is www.hootsuite.com.

> **CEO RESOURCE:**
> Social Media Scheduling Tool – *www.hootsuite.com*

Remember some good branding habits to employ here. Try to make sure that your brand name and tag line seemingly flow together like peanut butter and jelly. Also remember that short and concise is better with your brand name and tag line. Try to make your brand and tag line easy, catchy, and memorable. And lastly, remember that your USP does not need to portray that you're the best, just make sure that your USP shows why you are different and the right consumer choice.

CEO ACTIVITY:

- Block out one hour on your business calendar right now (7-14 days from now).
- List your company name and tag line and then ask yourself, "Do I think it is easy, catchy, and memorable?" Ask five others what they think to see where the business building activity should take you.
- Come up with three possible USPs. Ask other what they think.
- List what you want to be remembered for in the customer's mind and how that stands out from the rest.
- Start building around the data you collected.

BRAND LOYALTY

After building a strong brand and brand identity, the next step in a measurable leap forward is maximizing the opportunity to build *brand loyalty*. Some entrepreneurs focus all their attention on courting new customers. What they don't realize is that they can increase their profits by turning their happy customers into brand icons that shout their brand from the marketplace rooftops.

It is hard to gain new customers and, if not treated well post-sale, it is equally as hard to turn them into raving fans of your business. You could have a business income windfall by properly executing brand loyalty blueprints for your hard-earned new customers to follow. Some businesses don't focus on turning customers into raving fans because they are too worried about the next set of customers. This is a mistake! It is a huge business income opportunity lost, simply because when people are happy, that is the best time to cement their loyalty and ask for more.

<u>Why is building brand loyalty and brand champions so important?</u> A few reasons for putting your focus on building loyalty are the following:

- Because it is a fact that you will have some buyer's remorse. Building out the loyalty customer happiness funnel can help reduce buyer's remorse.
- Because newly secured customers that you build loyalty with can refer you more customers. (A warm independent referral is worth its weight in business-gold = Easier Sale.)
- Because not all customers will buy from you again, but a loyalty funnel can increase your repeat sales dramatically.
- Because you need nine consumers to equal one repeat buyer's revenue potential. (Source: Eric McEachern at <u>SweetToothRewards.com</u>)
- Because new customer conversion rates are 5 – 20% versus a repeat customer, which has an average conversion rate of 60 – 70%.

So, how do we start building brand loyalty?

- By asking for more, in the form of selling more products immediately post-sale, while brand loyalty is at its highest. Accomplish this with deeper discounts and incentives.
- By asking for customer referrals and incentivizing them.
- By asking them to boost your brand by giving a testimonial.
- By making them a brand spokesperson in some fashion to give notoriety.
- Give free shipping inducement for the next XX of months as a valuable new customer.

- Give them a private VIP customer service number that fast tracks wants and needs. This gives the feeling of specialized attention.
- Create a spotlight customer of the week or month to give them visibility.
- Give them VIP access prior to the public launch of new products and services.

Note: You will see more on the subject of _customer loyalty_ in chapter ten.

Creating brand loyalty can be as simple as going above and beyond your new customer's initial expectation. Offer happy customer service and perks (like free shipping) to cement their brand loyalty and let them bring more business to you.

Don't forget the power of a testimonial! It is simply a business fact that potential customers will always resonate with an independent endorsement of your products and services over your sales and marketing! Build loyalty that commands testimonials and it will pay dividends by uncovering "untapped new customer reach" that new customer marketing efforts could never match.

A brand slogan to live by to ensure you never lose brand loyalty focus is... "_Never ignore your happy customers for they are your best sales team!_"

> **CEO BIZ NON-NEGOTIABLE:** Super-Size Loyal Customers = A Referral Gold Rush!

Chapter 4:

Modernizing Your Business

21ST CENTURY BUSINESS ESSENTIALS

There is no question that if you want to build a 21st century business that lasts, then you need to make sure that you allocate a good amount of your *business building ON time* to modernizing your business. Whether you, as the CEO, want to admit it or not, times are changing. If your business is not poised to embrace change through modernization, then you've left a potentially gaping hole in your business suit-of-armor that the competition can, and will, pierce. Your more modern competition will use their better online reach, or easier sales efficiency, to take marketshare. To combat your competition, always make modernization a top priority.

It's a fact that most consumers today want your business to be available to them 24 hours a day. They want to consume your products and services when they want, which, with technology today, means that they are looking to make decisions to do business with you or your competitor not from nine to five, but rather 24 hours a day. The consumer universe is connected via the Internet. It goes with them in their pocket, on their tablets, and laptops everywhere they go.

Remember what we already discussed earlier. If you're hiding from the Internet your client will simply find someone else in 60 seconds, since your business is winking in the dark. This chapter is built on the foundation for taking purposeful steps to modernize your business and compete to win in today's endlessly-connected online marketplace.

MEET YOUR CUSTOMERS WHERE THEY LIVE! ONLINE!

Your customers come in all shapes and sizes, and it is sometimes hard to fit them all into one consumer box. However, there is one big box we can put them all in with a high degree of certainty: the "online consumer box." Within this box we can slice them into any number of categories. For this section, let's just classify consumers into two categories; the under-30 consumer and the over-30 consumer.

The under-30 consumer is 21st century battle-tested and seemingly wakes up with a high-speed Internet pipeline connected straight into their arm. It is almost like they are blinking into focus what they want via the Internet, without even leaving their bed in the morning. The other consumer bucket is the over-30 consumer, which does the exact same thing, whether they want to admit it or not. Yes, they may grab what they want a little slower than the under-30 consumer, but they still turn to technology and the Internet to get what they want. In fact, emarketer.com revealed that the average adult spent five hours and 38 minutes on the Internet per day. They also noted that the biggest increase in digital consumption was via mobile devices, which was roughly half of all daily digital usage. Hmmm… time to take your company digital!

"In today's online consumer jungle, interaction is the key to success!"

So if the consumer marketplace is organic (meaning a living organism) that is constantly growing, changing, and never sleeping, then the On-Purpose CEO needs to make sure that their business can meet their consumers when and where they consume... 24/7... Online. Remember, no more winking in the dark. Building a modern business, and keeping a modern business, is essential to staking your business claim versus your competition.

21ST CENTURY BUSINESS ESSENTIALS

If we are doing some modern business-building inventory, then we need to go down the list of items to make your brand nimble and digestible. We do this by dominating online while staying connected to current and future customers automatically. This means going from print and offline strategies to a digital brand, coupled with automation strategies to help you connect 24/7 in the consumer world. Print materials will always have a place in your marketing platform, but we need to modernize your company as well, and that starts with building your online presence.

What we really want to accomplish here is to have a company that produces opportunity and results while you sleep. After all, isn't it a wonderful thing to be able to grab attention, leads, and customers while you are resting for your next business growth move? Of course it is, and by staying up with current marketplace demands you gain the competitive edge that your business deserves.

GO DIGITAL OR GO HOME!

We need to look at your company to identify modern business opportunities that help you run your company, no matter how big or small. Let's start with your brand and logo graphics.

You can go online to find places that will create the brand images you will need to give your brand a boost. Two online examples for logo development or enhancement is www.fiverr.com and www.99designs.com. Use these to find excellent help to get your 21st century brand collateral in order. In fact, a designer on 99Designs.com created my logo for this brand and book.

You will need different file types and sizes for your logo and branding materials. For example, you might be trying to get your business website going and the logo file that you already have may not fit your website dimensions. If it fits your website, it might not fit your social media business pages (Facebook, Google+, Twitter).

Ask the person you hired to give you several different types of logo and marketing files to fit social profiles, brochure requirements, and website dimensions. This will save time by not having to backtrack and get items fixed later.

CEO RESOURCE:

Virtual Assistant Services *www.fiverr.com*
Logo Design Help *www.99designs.com*

WEBSITES: OPEN FOR BIZ 24/7

You should have a website set up that embodies your company, brand and USP. If done right, this can be your 24-hour sales pitch. Remember that today's consumers have been trained to search for what they want online. They have been trained to expect the search will yield what they want, instantly. This is why it is critical to have your branded, best website.

The beauty of modernizing your business with your website is that it becomes your 24-hour-a-day brand homing beacon that can:

- Convey your brand's Unique Selling Proposition.
- House your business welcome video to connect consumers with your branding and business story.
- Capture customers while you sleep.
- Convey your business "Mission Statement."
- Convey your products and services.
- Connect with consumers when they want to connect 24/7/365.

In today's world of push button technology, establishing a website is much easier than you think. I want to address this because most new business owners, and even established business owners, think that creating a real business website is going to cost thousands of dollars and be very complicated. That is not true. You can get a website set up very inexpensively that looks professional. The bigger concern is to set one up that has real functionality and is on a flexible platform that can be easily tweaked from time-to-time. Probably the most popular website platform today is the WordPress platform.

Setting up a website can be as easy as going to www.templatemonster.com and picking a website theme. Hire someone from a virtual assistant website to build out the specifics for you. It is really that simple.

I can hear you asking, "What am I going to say on my website?" TextBroker.com is a website with professional writers that work very cheaply to build your content for marketing, websites, mission statements, press releases and more. As an example, I had a press release written and it only cost eight dollars total. Trust me, it was way better than anything that I could have written, and it was done in less than 48 hours.

CEO RESOURCE: Pick website themes.

www.templatemonster.com

> CEO RESOURCE: *www.textbroker.com* to have professionals write your content for as little as five to ten dollars at a time. You tell them what you are thinking and they will turn your ideas into a well-written masterpiece.

ONLINE DIRECTORY PLACE-MARKING

You business website is obviously not the only spot on the Internet. Therefore, there must be other places that consumers have become accustomed to visiting on the Internet for information. To help get your business noticed, you should add your business to _online directories_ such as Google and Yahoo. This helps your business pop up faster when consumers are searching online. The more places you register your business and brand online, the faster you start to rise in the search results for your business niche.

Important Competition Notice: As you start to get a larger online footprint, your competition is going to notice. Here is the potential business problem. If you have not cemented your business registration in the different *online directories,* then the competition can register in those directories under your business name and redirect those customers to their products and services.

I'm quite certain that if you knew your competitors were profiting off of your hard work to grow your brand, that you might blow a business-gasket. Nobody wants to get put in business time out, so make sure that you add registering in online directories to your business agenda.

> CEO RESOURCE: *www.knowem.com* - Online Directory Business Placement Service

> **CEO Tip:** You can hire people that are online directory experts to register your company, so competitors do not steal your future customers.

GETTING SOCIAL!

A modern business is a SOCIAL business! With the explosion of the information technology highway, reaching others has never been easier. In fact, reaching an audience of your potential customers today is a million times easier than even ten years ago. One of the biggest ways to grow your customer base is utilizing social sharing websites. I love it because you can grow your business without leaving your couch!

I call it, "The No Gas Money Spent Program!"
— Jason Palliser

One of the biggest sections of the information technology explosion has been social sharing websites such as Facebook, LinkedIn, and Twitter, to name a few.

Not going social is NOT an option for an On-Purpose CEO. Why, you might ask? It is real simple to explain. Imagine knowing that ¾ of the world is going to be at a daily meeting and you purposefully decide (as a smart business decision – *joking*) to ignore ¾'s of the world's consumers. You wouldn't do that. Now, let's point out that you can reach this audience without even having to spend any gas money. Do you think that it might be the RIGHT business decision to get social? Of course it is not only the right decision, it is also the smart decision for your modern business.

"Your business isn't in your office; it lives in the minds you meaningfully touch!"

Another big reason "getting social" is *so* important is that these social sites are authority websites, which means they give your business monster online-mojo when it comes to your rankings on other search engines. When consumers are searching across all different types of search engines, your presence on "authority websites" (websites with millions of visitors) makes you rank higher in search results.

You see, it is not just about the social sites you are setting up your business presence on, it is also about how your business is being set up on these sites to get you more exposure outside of those social platforms. "Search engines," such as Google, Yahoo, Bing, and more, recognize that your business is essentially everywhere; therefore your business must be more relevant than your competitors who have not spread their online footprint across relevant social platforms. Lastly, the more social engagement you have on these social sites, the more online recognition you get from all of the search engines. By engaging on social platforms you are ranked higher than your competition.

Some staples to cement your social presence on are Facebook, LinkedIn, and Twitter, just to name a few. Again, these are authority websites. Facebook is the second ranked authority website in the world. YouTube is the third ranked website in the world. LinkedIn is the first ranked business website in the US and Canada. The more determined you are to branch out on these social sites, the more reach you'll have and the higher you'll rank when consumers search for your products and services.

One key component, when setting up your business on these social sites, is to make sure you put in a *strong profile* about your business. Tell the world exactly who you are and exactly what you do or provide, and absolutely let them know how to reach you. DO NOT make it hard to get in touch with you.

The whole reason you are building an online footprint for your company is to attract customers, business partners, or both. Place your e-mail, website, and phones numbers within your profiles to make doing business with you easy! You may want to hire a virtual assistant to set these up for you. You can hire one from websites like www.fiverr.com or www.upwork.com. Simply place an ad for the help you need and ask them to send you their qualifications.

SPECIAL NOTE:

One of the most valuable pieces of advice given to me was by a very successful businessman named Kevin Short. He told me, "Jason, the only thing standing in your way to building a great business is you!" This man buys, builds, and sells businesses across the country. He basically told me not to stand in my own way for progress. The company is only as valuable as your willingness to let it be. A shorter version of this would be to say, "Get out of your own way!" You know, right now, that your business could be even bigger than it is today, so take steps to make it happen and put the right pieces in place to help automate and modernize your business. Show the business world why they should take notice.

NO MORE WINKING IN THE DARK!

FAQS

Use your FAQ's as a consumer objection hammer to squash their doubts about doing business with you! Use it to your advantage as a page on your website, as a flyer to give to prospective customers, and as an auto-responder message to get more new clients. Again, it is time to make your business life easier and the life of your future customers easier as well. My suggestions is to perform this business task in a word document or mind map. Use this later to create your new website content, email responses, and flyers.

> **CEO ACTIVITY:** Develop your Top Ten Most Frequently Asked Questions or FAQs
>
> - Take 15-30 minutes to brainstorm on the top ten Frequently Asked Questions by consumers and type out the answers to those questions.
> - Add this list of FAQ's to your website, so it can help gain more customers and also shorten the buying decision time frame!

AUTOMATE YOUR BUSINESS

Your modernized business would not be complete without exploring some options to help you automate. Remember that technology is your business friend and not your business foe. That said, you can't do it alone. Trying will leave you working too hard *in* your business, rather than automating some business items to keep you working *on* your business (like an On-Purpose CEO).

CRM

The beauty of building a 21st century business is that there are many tools to help you take your business income to a whole new level with less effort. One of the most important ways to help automate your business is to implement a lead capture and lead tracking system. You can do this by searching online to find a good *Customer Relationship Management or CRM*

Tool to help you run your business. There are tons of them in the marketplace to choose from. At a minimum, choose a CRM that has the following features:

- Lead Capture System
- Auto-Responders for Follow Up Campaigns
- Automatic Lead Tagging and Categorizing
- Mass E-mail Capabilities (Mail Merging)
- Easy Contact Importing and Exporting
- Lead Capture Page Creation Functions

The key here is to understand that you can automate the lead and customer experience. This can give you monster leverage because you can be out of town, on vacation, interviewing a new employee, or whatever, while the CRM is giving your new leads the helpful information necessary to close the deal. The best part? All of this is happening independent of your time and energy. _Massive Leverage_!

As an example, wouldn't you like to be able to have a potential customer fill out a form on your website and automatically get a nice e-mail back from you and your company with a list of your FAQ's? Of course you would! They may be ready to buy as soon as you or your team gets on the phone with them. Or better yet, you could have the FAQ's and a purchase link inside the e-mail, so therefore you can close the sale "hands-free."

So what has happened here? You've started modernizing your business, and you are now obtaining new lead prospects hands-free, as well as helping them make an "Easier / User-Friendly" decision to become your next customer. Furthermore, you can now collect and sort your customers with one or two clicks. With the right CRM organizing everything for you, you can easily send your next business offering or opportunity. This is a business home run. Let the system do the heavy lifting for you.

The tracking functions of your CRM are a next-level way to see where your marketing efforts are winning or failing. They give you real insight into what you may need to change or tweak to get the results you want. This is invaluable to helping you see where you should focus your CEO efforts. This is a big business step towards building your best business "On Purpose!"

"A Good CRM is your business income growth crystal ball!" -Jason Palliser

The other not-so-apparent reason you want to utilize a platform to run your best business through is that it can raise the value of your business in the eyes of others (future potential buyers). In other words, it makes your business more attractive to others. Having an engine that can prove where you are getting customers from, show how your customers are responding, does all the follow up work, as well as content organization can increase the value of your business immensely! Why? Because a prospective buyer of your business can see they are buying a successful, streamlined, turnkey operation. You may want to sell in the future, so modernize now to increase your attractiveness and sales price.

> **CEO To-Do Item:** Research and implement a good CRM to run your business!

> **CEO Resource:** Which CRM is right for your business? Check out this questionaire.
>
> BiggerBusinessBlueprint.com/CRMHelp

GO FROM DEPENDENT TO INDEPENDENT!

All too often I see business owners that have problems taking their business income to the next level. One common denominator I typically see is that they have not slowed down to put a deliberate workflow process in place (documenting all of their resources and processes). This would allow them to grow easier with digestible marching orders. They lack real leverage!

It is human nature to want to be involved in every part of the process. Especially when it comes to your personal business. The brutal fact though, is that you are probably the one that is holding your business back because every decision and every resource is dependent on you. The business is co-dependent on you, and that is one of your largest bottlenecks inhibiting your growth.

There are a few things you can do to help break through this self-imposed income glass ceiling. Your income will spike if we can give you business independence. First is _centralizing your business_ by taking all of the business resources and contacts out of your head and catalog them in a centralized location (hopefully in a CRM that can be accessed online).

By doing this you are poising your business to take the next growth step. It will be easy for you and your growing team to grab what they need effortlessly, without being dependent on you, which in turn allows for growth independent of you. You should not be the only one that can make the call to your supplier to order more products. You should not be the only one with the information to verify that the shipment will be on time. The only way this can happen is to catalog, categorize, and publish your resources centrally for others to access. This leaves you free to work on your next big product, offering, or other income initiatives.

While you are centralizing, now is a good time to take the documentation to the next level by not only documenting vital resources, but also cataloging what the normal cost is for each resource. This eliminates guesswork and mistakes when you offload the responsibilities to others. This is what I call *"adding the metrics"* for business streamlining. Take it even deeper by attaching the *right people to talk to* with each resource to reduce the time to get the task accomplished.

This process is what I call, *"Turing the intangible into the tangible,"* because people cannot touch your thoughts, but they can digest your vision when it is on paper for others to follow and consume. If you ever really want your business to grow for you with less of your valuable time invested, then this step is critical to achieving your best "On Purpose" business.

Once you have done as much documenting as you can to poise your business for growth, *now it is time to outsource as much as you possibly can.* This will free you, as the On-Purpose CEO, to perform the *High Dollar Productive Activities* that creates income and growth spikes for your company.

An easy way to help you start the process is to ask yourself the question, "Can I have someone else do this, and if I document the processes well, can they do it as well as me?" If the answer is yes, then you need to look to outsource the business task or process. The faster you do this, the faster you will grow your bank account.

> **CEO Activity:** Five Ways To Modernize Your Business
>
> - Take five to ten minutes and come up with at least five ways you can modernize your business in the next 30-45 days.
> - Schedule 30 minutes to brainstorm what each modernization solution will take to accomplish, and then prioritize the steps.

Set a hard start and finish date for each new component to be accomplished and schedule them on your business calendar. Share with your team and your business partners, so that everyone knows the expectations you've set for your company. Plus, your partners, employees, investors, and others appreciate when they can see you are spearheading purposeful change to help grow the business. This makes company buy-in much easier.

Chapter 5:

The Perfect Customer

BEFORE YOU CAN GRAB THE PERFECT CUSTOMERS, YOU NEED TO UNDERSTAND YOUR PERFECT CUSTOMER!

We have all heard the phrase, "The customer is always right!" While that may or may not be true, there is one thing that is true: "Anyone can _have a business_, but not everyone can be _in_ business!" Why? Because _you can be a business on paper_, _but that does not mean you are in business_. To be in business you need customers! If you want to get the sale, which is one of the most critical aspects to being in business, then you need to create a winning customer formula.

It has never been easier to attract potential customers because of the connective power of the Internet. Yet, _with the Internet's easy attraction, comes easy distraction,_ so building the best customer acquisition battle plan is even more critical to your business success. You need to build your ideal customer persona profile, and create a marketing plan specific to them.

Once we have zeroed-in on our perfect customer profile, we then need to map out the best customer acquisition strategies. These strategies must mirror the buying process traits of our perfect customer, and then fight like hell to keep them once we have them. In this chapter we will break down everything about the perfect customer, which is the lifeblood of any business... so let's build your best customer acquisition war chest using the skills you will learn in this chapter!

GOING DEEP WITH THE CUSTOMER...

Knowing about your customer is really the tip of the business-growth iceberg. Knowing their wants and needs - on the deepest level – will help you surpass your competition. To understand your customer the deepest requires digging into the customer demographics, their buying tendencies, their buying cycles, and knowing the best ways to keep them once you get them. We are going to attack the "understanding the perfect customer persona" discovery process just like we would attack eating an elephant... one bite at a time.

WHO IS YOUR CUSTOMER? [PERSONA]

Building your best customer marketing and branding plan is accomplished when you dissect the persona of your ideal customer or client. As you start to build your best customer profile, you want to focus on a few key areas. You want to understand the demographic of the customer, the mind and/or psychographic profile of your customer, and their tendencies. This will help you zero-in on the best place to find and capture your coveted perfect customer. Once you've defined the above, then you can better understand their tendencies and behaviors to better locate what customer sandboxes they play in. This will maximize your lead potential.

PERFECT CUSTOMER DEMOGRAPHIC

Start by asking yourself, "*What demographic best describes my perfect customer?*" Write down as many characteristics as you can to use later as lead capture gold. Is your perfect customer young (under 30) or are they older (over 50 – 55)? As you probably are starting to see, the better you are at deeply understanding who your perfect customers are, the easier it becomes to market to and serve them better. This is the way to grow your business, increase your business profits, and clearly stand out from the competition.

Sample Criteria to Define:

- Age
- Gender or Gender Neutral – Most offerings typically favor one gender or the other.
- Income Level
- Marital Status
- Ethnic Background
- Religious Beliefs
- Location / Geographic

Here is why the demographic is so important. If your products and services cater to an older crowd, then it only makes sense that you attack the places where older potential customers live, breathe, and gather. Doesn't that make sense? If your product is Recreational Vehicle sales or RVs, then you should probably build marketing and branding around seeing the countryside and traveling the USA during retirement. You probably shouldn't target college campuses with your marketing initiatives to grab RV purchaser leads. This is why the demographic dissection of your perfect customer is critical to your business growth success.

Again, the key here is to go as deep as you can when defining the demographic of your target customer. If you are going really deep, then you need to look beyond the normal age, gender, and income demographics. Dig deeper by trying to determine typicality like marital status, religious beliefs, geographical location, and ethnic background (to name a few). To really dig deep, I suggest blocking out an hour and do it with a team of three or four people (or more if you want). Have everyone think of everything they can about the perfect customer.

Once you've put that in writing, rank each trait in order of highest importance to lowest importance. This will be invaluable later when you develop your USP and your marketing material. Now you can build around the high value items to attract your best target customer. Performing this critical business initiative is a giant step towards building your best "On Purpose Business" customer acquisition plan.

PERFECT CUSTOMER PSYCHOGRAPHICS

Now that the demographic is nailed down, it is time to turn our focus on getting into the mind of our perfect target customer. As we start to dig deeper into our perfect customer profile, we now want to enter their mind to try to understand what their buying triggers are on a cerebral level.

Knowing how our perfect target customer thinks is the key to grabbing the most customers that you can as an On-Purpose CEO. If you know how they think, then you can start to anticipate what their biggest buying triggers may be. With their behavior decoded, you can build a war chest of nasty ninja marketing hooks to land the customer.

Sample Criteria to Define:

- Personality type: extrovert, introvert, cautious, carefree, happy, sad, etc.
- Preferences

- Attitude
- Lifestyle
- Sense of being

The psychographic part of your customer dissection centers on what their personality traits are. Once we have zeroed-in on their personality traits, we can now start to add more game changing characteristics to our perfect customer persona. Preferences can be attitudes, lifestyle models, and the overall sense of being for that personality type, which can unlock mounds of new customers that help you make wheelbarrows of cash.

EXAMPLE:

Let's use "Gamers or Video Game Junkies" as a good example of why customer personality modeling is critical to your business success and longevity. Hypothetically, you and your top two competitors are fighting to get customers in the gaming community. Your competitors have chosen to market by delivering the latest and greatest game to the market at the lowest price.

Your target customer research is better than your competitors and as a result you are in the mind of the gamers. Your psychographic analysis has helped you develop the USP (marketing hook) that is not centered on price, but rather on their competitive nature. This target customer is worried less about price and more about getting their hands on the product first. They are WILLING TO PAY MORE TO GET IT FIRST because they are competitive and don't want spoilers to ruin the experience. Your company capitalizes on this by guaranteeing they get first crack at the game or they get 10% of the purchase price back as a discount.

That is a target customer persona victory. Not only are you taking potential customers away from your competitors, you are making more money at the same time! He or she who builds the best customer persona WINS!

> **CEO Tip:** To understand your customer better, practice putting yourself in their shoes and go through the motions of buying your own products and services. This may uncover some weaknesses in your offerings and/or process that were invisible until you put yourself in their shoes!

PERFECT CUSTOMER TENDENCIES AND BEHAVIOR PATTERNS

Now that you have taken your perfect customer approach to a much deeper level, you can now look to attach their behavior and tendencies to round out the perfect customer persona. If you have adopted the policy to understand our perfect customer better than anyone one on Earth, then it should only be logical that you can anticipate their purchasing patterns and behaviors.

Sample Criteria to Define:

- Are they loyal?
- Are they fickle?
- Are they motivated with rewards?
- Do they just want the best price right now?
- Will they pay more to belong to something bigger than the product or service itself?

You can now meld your business USP and marketing/sales plans into the perfect lead acquisition weapon to stand out from the competition and win new clients with surgical-like precision. No grabbing customers *on accident*. You are grabbing customers *on purpose* because you know exactly who they are, where they are, what they want, and their buying behaviors. In the marketing world that is like taking a test, yet having the answers to the test before the it even starts. Knowing your perfect customer persona is your absolute and utterly unfair advantage.

Knowing their behaviors like loyalty patterns (or lack there of) and if they are 'price' versus 'reward-based' buyers can generate loads of business income. This knowledge results in spending much less on marketing, which is the true internal business win-win for any growing company.

CUSTOMER ACQUISITION

On the way to building your best "On Purpose Business" we need to make sure your customer acquisition process is tested, tracked, and refined. One of the biggest mistakes business owners make today is to just throw out a big marketing blanket and hope to get results, when they know there is no rhyme or reason to what they are doing. The only way to truly build a modern rock-solid customer acquisition strategy is to track everything. Only then can you flip the income light switch back on and build our customer base with clear business intelligence.

The first aspect of customer acquisition to investigate is the method in which you grab prospective clients. Do you grab clients via billboards, area event sponsorships, phone applications, bulk mailers, skywriting, or any combination of these and other methods?

The prudent way to approach this aspect of building your business is to map out your current methods of new customer acquisition and exhaust the question: "*How can I make this*

process better and find new ways to pick up new customers?"
Focusing on new ways to improve your customer acquisition,
coupled with developing new test strategies to pick up even
more customers, is one of the most powerful business building
activities you'll ever perform. (*In later chapters we will discuss
a multitude of lead generation strategies to test and implement,
as well as discuss different ways to get business leverage to help
with customer acquisition strategies.*)

CEO ACTIVITY: As a business building exercise, I
want you to list out all of the ways you currently
grab new customers, or if your business is new, then
list the ways you plan to attack customer acquisition.
Your next step of this process is to apply a dollar
cost per acquisition of each new client. You may
have never tried to track/quantify this part of your
business process before. The reason is simple. You
need to know with a high degree of certainty what
you are spending to get new customers in the door.

Later we will talk in more detail how to use some tools to track
your customer acquisition costs. The better you can become
at tracking your costs per customer, the easier it will become
to make and budget marketing decisions that have a positive
impact on the profitability of your business.

CEO ACTIVITY: Five New Ideas To Grab Customers

* Spend five minutes and flip on the creative switch
  in your business brain to expand your customer
  acquisition dragnet.

The key here is not to limit yourself. You need to write down
any idea to grab new customers that you think you might try

or want to try. Don't worry about the business growth killer that lurks in your brain whispering, "How are you going to have time to do all of this?" We will put that monster in its place with leverage strategies in chapter eight!

CUSTOMER SALES CYCLE

Building a bulletproof customer acquisition plan should also take the typical sales cycle process and typical nature of the sale into consideration. The fact is that different products command different approaches to get the best customer acquisition results. Due to the type of product/service you are selling, your process for the sale may be longer or shorter. In fact, understanding that you may be taking too long to get the sale, or trying to get the sale too quick, can unlock massive income potential for your products and services.

As an example, maybe your product is a luxury car, which involves customers spending a large part of their income to buy your product. This is typically a longer sales cycle, which involves a lot more thought on the part of your potential customer than buying a hat. So, in the spirit of putting into motion what you are learning in this book, you can start to test your sales process. Try adding an extra customer-acquisition nurturing step or two to get them more ready to buy. This could dramatically increase your sales percentages.

On the flip side, your product may be the newest all-purpose cleaner on the market and you may have 101 reasons why it is the best cleaner you will ever own, but your sales suffer because the sales process is too long. This is where you may want to remove barriers to purchase and experience a large sales increase as a result. The important business item to note here is that you need to test the sales buying cycle to see where you experience the biggest gains. Implement your findings into all of your sales process maps and funnels.

Another example to illustrate my point is to consider holiday sale items. These are more seasonal purchases. Typically the business sales, if mapped out on a graph, would look like a carnival rollercoaster with spikes and dips in product sales. Knowing this, you may want to implement a plan that adds one or two additional items to the sales funnel and employs a sales strategy of "getting a jump on your next holiday" where you add merchandise that solves their next holiday crisis. I would go with a strategy to increase sales by having customers buy before they even contemplate buying in the future. I can test out sales by saying, "We know holidays keep you busy, click here for a *Stress-Free Easter*" and have them buy holiday décor for a couple of holidays instead of one.

Factors to Consider:

- Is the sales process long or short?
- Are there typically repeat sales?
- What is the nature of the sale? Necessity, Convenience, Luxury, Impulse, Gift, Holiday, etc.

Is the sale item typically a repeat item? If so, then offer in bulk to get more sales. Test out a few different offerings to settle into your sales sweet spot. An article from RJMetrics.com noted that your chances of getting future business from new customers in the first year is roughly 32%, which means that your should try to get as much in product sales upfront as you possibly can from the new customer because they may not be back after the initial sale.

Another interesting statistic from the 18 million+ consumers that RJMetrics.com collects data from: roughly 69% of what they will spend with your company on an annual basis comes within their first 30 days of being your customer. What does that mean to you from a sales perspective? *Strike while the new customer iron is HOT!* The smart way to maximize your income is to focus your efforts on getting even more products offered and sold within the first 30 days of acquiring a customer. This is your best chances of getting the most out of your hard-fought customer.

The top one percent of your online customers are typically worth 18 times more than your average customer. I strongly suggest implementing a push for more sales early in the new client phase to maximize conversion from new client to *best* client. It only makes sense that you *take the time to put together the world's greatest client retention program known to mankind* to increase the likelihood of oozing mounds of business cash flow from your *current customer base*.

CEO RESOURCE: Need more help with building a sales funnel? Visit:

BiggerBusinessBlueprint.com/FunnelHelp

CUSTOMER RETENTION AND LOYALTY

There is a mountain of cash hidden inside your current customer database. It can be unlocked with the implementation of a strong customer retention and customer loyalty program. *Building income from within your customer base can turn a good business into a great business*. It is all too common that I see business owners focusing on customer acquisition only, and they are missing out on the income benefits that come with a good customer retention plan. Backup the value truck and deliver the best retention/loyalty plan you can to command a spike in your business profits.

"Privately connect with your customers well; they'll praise you publically!" - Unknown

A great way to grow your business is to not lose customers. If you do all you can to be a retention champion, then you may create loyal customers for life. Loyal customers can bring you the holy grail of business, which is referring you new customers who are pre-sold via brand loyalty. This is business gold.

Growing your business, via loyal customers and brand advocates, starts with building your best customer retention program. *You did something right! They bought from you! An On-Purpose CEO knows that the post-sale process is an amazing way to keep income flowing virtually forever.*

There are several ways to build your customer retention plan. It starts with simply following up with them. Several publications in the marketing and business growth space publish that it takes an average of seven or more touch points with a prospect before they buy. That follow up is critical to the sales success of a business. The post-sales process is no different.

Your best customer retention plan starts with building a follow up plan to enhance their buying experience, reduce buyer's remorse, anchor future product sales, and build brand loyalty. An On-Purpose CEO will set time aside to scout their competitors and dig into their follow up funnels and post-sale funnels to develop the best strategy.

Sample Retention Strategies
- Customer Appreciation Hooks
- Customer Spotlight
- Loyalty Program with Benefits
- VIP Service Offerings
- Guarantees (with or without time limits)

Customer retention should be a major part of your business focus. I should also note here that I am not speaking of just repeat sales, but also of complimentary sales as well. Almost every product or service has complimentary sales that could be attached to it and you should be able to profit from them. A great way to tap into this source of business income is to anchor it into your customer retention process.

Deploying your retention plan helps you circle the wagons around your new customer. You fought hard to get the attention of your new customer. You fought against competition to earn their business. Now, don't lose them because you shuffled them aside after the sale with lack of proper customer attention.

There is no better time than the present to kick-start your retention efforts. Right after the sale your new customer can get buyer's remorse. Your effort to confirm they made the right buying decision rests squarely upon your business shoulders. Maximizing the customer value starts by reconfirming they have made the right choice by doing some of the following retention efforts:

- Sending over a customer purchase survey.
- Implementing a Thank You call program.
- Recognizing them on your website and/or social media pages. (Ex: Welcome to the family!)
- Send them a card.
- Give them discount specials.
- Confirm their order.
- Confirm their shipment and/or appointment.
- Make them a VIP Customer.
- Notify them that they are now in your rewards program.
- Give them satisfaction guarantees.
- Give them VIP perks such as Expedited Service and/or Preferred Pricing.
- Send them customer appreciation coupons.
- Enter them into customer contests for free "stuff."
- Activate them into your business follow up drip campaign.
- Educate them more about your products and business.

You must stay in touch with your customers or you are out of touch with the most vital part of your business success. Educate them on your business, products, and services to reaffirm they are in the right spot. Strengthen your position with your customers to keep the competition a distant speck in your rear view mirror.

> "Great Execution is the Ultimate Differentiator."
> – Margaret Molloy

Bringing customers to your business offering, to the buying finish line, and _through_ the sale with retention value hooks, is the _business-road-less-traveled_! It can widen the gap between you and your competitors. Garnering happy customers is not an accident; in fact it is done on purpose. _Putting your retention plan in writing is something that 90% of your competitors don't do because they are busy guessing where they are going to get their next customer_. Use their un-organization to your business advantage by building a value path from their company to yours, which is reinforced by your well-thought-out customer retention, satisfaction, and loyalty plan.

CEO ACTIVITY:

Use the top ten FAQ's you created about your company in chapter four and add them to your follow up drip campaign. These "Did you know" items will help cement your relationship and loyalty as well as provide opportunities to sell additional products or services.

CEO RESOURCE: Need more help with a customer loyalty program? Visit:

BiggerBusinessBlueprint.com/LoyaltyHelp

"Circle the wagons around your new customers! You worked hard to get them, so don't forget them!"

– Jason Palliser

Chapter 6:

Business Marketing and Sales

BUILDING THE BETTER MARKETING MOUSE TRAP!

"Marketing is no longer about the stuff that you make, but about the stories you tell." – Seth Godin

Marketing and sales are the lifeblood of any company. Without sales, any company will wither and die. To get sales, we need to market to our perfect customer persona and speak to them with our marketing. With the advent of the Internet today, we have to go a step further. We have to speak to our perfect customer *well* with our marketing. Information is *so* readily available today that it is not even close to good enough just to get "information" out there about your products and services. You need to "Market Well" to get sales and take marketshare away from your competitors.

In this chapter you will learn about all the components that make up a great marketing message, while keeping in mind that today's consumers are social and want to connect to the story about "your stuff" just as much as they want what your "stuff" offers. You will learn to build marketing with purposeful sales triggers that compete and win against the competition in the online and offline business jungle. You will also look at the marketing paths available to increase you desired results.

MARKETING MESSAGE PREFACE

Before we dig into the meat and potatoes of crafting your marketing messaging, I want to put two caveats around this section. If you can keep these two rules in mind as you build your marketing message, you'll strike marketing gold.

DON'T FORGET WHO YOUR AUDIENCE IS.

You've already put in the time to understand your perfect customer persona, so now it is time to build marketing collateral that commands the attention of your most desired customer. Take all of the items you know to be true about your perfect target customer, and build your ads to gain and keep their attention from the headline all the way down to your specific marketing call-to-action.

KEEP IT SIMPLE!

> "If you can't explain it to a 6-year old, you don't know it yourself." – Albert Einstein

One of the biggest marketing principles to live by is to become a better marketer by making your marketing message simple and to the point. Use words sparingly because if there is too much going on, then you've already lost your potential customer.

While you are trying to keep it simple, also be aware of the tone your marketing messages are conveying. Make sure the tone of your marketing message matches the target customer persona of your audience. It needs to deliver the feeling you want to emote in your perfect customer persona, which exudes their views and tendencies. The better you become at delivering the right tone in your marketing, the faster you can build your customer generating super-engine. Match your marketing efforts to your perfect customer persona by applying the right action triggers (versus trying to get too cute with your marketing plans). The right tone and message can motivate prospects to turn into sales. The bottom line is that simple is better.

MARKETING MESSAGE KEY COMPONENTS

Building a better marketing message has some key components to consider. Most business owners do not touch several of these marketing components, therefore not all marketing is created equal!

Most business owners view the marketing process as a necessary chore that they would like to complete as fast as possible because it is not their cup of tea. But if you build your marketing campaigns with the right components in place, your marketshare will grow.

HEADLINES

"8 out of 10 consumers will ready the headline copy, but only 2 out of 10 will read the rest!"
– CopyBlogger

"Headlines are worth 90% of the advertising dollar!"
– David Ogilvy

Poor headlines inside your marketing can be the gatekeeper holding your income hostage! Why? Because lack of powerful headlines in your marketing, as you see from the quotes above, may be pushing away eight out of ten potential customers!

If we are looking to put your best marketing foot forward, then we need to start with *creating powerful headlines*! You need to address the headline. When I say headline, I mean the headline for online ad placement, the title of your print ads, and your e-mail subject lines.

The headline has to be powerful enough to capture their attention or they are already gone. Your window of opportunity in today's digital world is short, so you have to be razor sharp with a catchy, interesting, and action-provoking headline to get your potential lead to read your entire message. You can have the best offer in the world, but if you cannot capture their attention, then it doesn't matter if your offer is a showstopper. They will never get to read the punch line. Your lack of headline pizzazz will allow the competition to get the sale.

Headlines win customers! Make the headline sizzle and strike a cord with the reader's curiosity. Build a headline that commands them to dig deeper.

Here are some headline writing tips to try:

- Using numbers in your headline.
- Use catchy adjectives.
- Use triggering words like "why," "how," or "when."
- Add a mega-promise.
- Make sure it is ultra-useful or mega-specific.

Try adding most of these together to create better headlines:

Ex #1: How to prepare awesome dinners! (A little bland, huh?)

Ex #2: 12 Lightning fast ways to create empty dinner plates every time! (You feel the difference, don't you?)

> **CEO Non-Negotiable:** Scout the competition before you hit "go" on your marketing! Find interesting headlines and make yours slap the crap out of theirs!

Headline Creation Tips:

- Google "Best Headlines."
- Go to competitors and research their marketing.
- Create a marketing folder and drop interesting ads in there to use later.
- Google "Ad Words" to research popular buzzwords/ phrases for your specific type of lead.

PERSONALIZE

The next step of your marketing transformation is to _talk to the lead more personally_. When they open your marketing offer (ad or e-mail), try to address them personally by using verbiage like Dear, Fellow, Hey Smart Buyer, and other similar welcoming terms. You are putting them at ease to dig deeper into your marketing. Remember that they can leave whenever they want, so you have to keep them engaged.

INSIDE HEADLINE

The next marketing component to consider is adding another headline inside your ad/marketing message. _Time to keep_ *them interested!* You've got them to swallow the bait, so now you want to sink the hook by reminding them of why they are there. Do this by restating the headline or add another one that embodies the essence of your commanding message.

The key here is to mentally sink the hook they bit even deeper by keeping the interest at a zenith. You don't have to do this, but it is a strong suggestion. This is where you can also introduce your USP or Unique Selling Proposition, which separates you from the rest of the competition and starts to lead them towards the sale.

HOOK

As they dive into the first line of your marketing ad, this is the spot where you want to try to *Hook* them into your products and services by making a polite *Emotional Plea* or in other words, _show them that you identify with them_. One of the best practices to accomplish this is to hit them in their pain or pleasure centers by telling them you know how they feel. After all, didn't you spend the time to get to know your perfect customer? So show them you are in their shoes!

Can you say, "Cha-Ching!" This is where you are hitting them with the first buying trigger. You are emotionally connecting with your target audience. The decision to "BUY" is an emotional one, so you are showing them right out of the marketing gate that you know how they feel and you are here to help. Your goal here is to anchor them to you because finally they have something that they identify with. This is brand success when you can accomplish this through marketing and sales objectives.

BENEFITS

Now we get to the meat and potatoes portion of your marketing ads and messages. With your headlines, endearments, and emotional plea, you've set the stage for your _offer and benefits._ Your marketing has hooked them in deeper, so now it is time to solve their problem or needs with your strong product offer and benefits.

The best way to make your pitch is to _Paint a Story!_ Here is where you will tell them how your offering benefits them and how your offering is unique... to walk them closer to the sale. Remember that "marketing stuff" folder I told you to create? Use that content as a resource to paint a good story around your product offering that moves your prospects towards the sale.

A tip to help you write a better offer is to keep in mind that people think in terms of pictures. Make sure that whatever your ad says, it paints the picture you want in the mind of your future buyer. It is your CEO duty to be better at painting the right story with your offer.

As an example, let's say you are trying to sell a house and you put your marketing out into the consumer marketplace by saying the following:

"Freshly renovated 3 bedroom and 2 bath with a finished basement. It has a fenced in yard and is close to a park."

It is a description, but it really does not evoke a ton of emotions that would lead to action.

But how about painting a picture...

"You're going to love your new home; especially while making dinner in your new kitchen and watching the kids play in the park right across the street. The dog will love the fenced-in yard. We even built a man-cave in the basement, so you can throw your husband down there and enjoy the rest of this 3 bed and 2 bath house. Move in worry-free, and love the fact that you can go from highway to couch in less than two minutes."

Your words can turn into weapons when you paint the picture to help the prospects feel and breathe your products and services. Get inside their heads and paint the perfect sales picture that commands they become your next customer!

CALL TO ACTION

If done properly, you've brought your perfect customer to the marketing finish line, which is the USP and Call to Action! *Getting the sale ends with your specific Call to Action.* You've captured their interest, you kept their interest, you've piqued their interest, and now it is time to go in for the lead-capture-kill with your Call to Action.

The call to action has to be better than your competition or you will lose business and potential clients. This is where your Unique Selling Proposition comes into play. The potential lead is at the marketing finish line and they are deciding to contact you or not, so *give them a reason* to contact you. Hit them with the big *Why You* proposition via a commanding USP.

To reel them in, politely add in a little scarcity to your compelling plea to contact you, such as, "the first 100 get this discounted offer," or "while inventory lasts," or "48 hour window to get the extra XYZ with your purchase!" There has to be a compelling plea to make sure they do not leave without taking action towards the sale.

I always tell my business clients that they have to solve the "I'll do it tomorrow" syndrome with their USP and call to action – because chances are they won't do it tomorrow, either. Blow their mind with your call to action, which should be easy since you've taken the time to understand your perfect customer persona.

> **CEO TIP:** Depending on what type of marketing you are doing, consider adding some sort of "P.S." message at the end of your marketing because it can be your get out of jail free card. Hit them with your most important sales hook or USP before they go. Why use a P.S.? Because everyone reads them, so use it to your marketing advantage!

> **CEO RESOURCE:** If you have a hard time coming up with marketing messages, because admittedly you are not that creative, then have someone else do it for you. It is business money well spent! Trust me! Hire a professional that lives and breathes "Hooks, Headlines, and Calls to Action" on a daily basis. It is what they do, so utilize their skill set to make more money. Here's a tool to help you come up with marketing materials and sales copy by just answering questions... You're Welcome!

> **CEO RESOURCE:** Get sales copy help: *scriptdoll.net* Answer questions about your products and services and let it create the copy and marketing foundations for you!

PUT YOUR BEST MARKETING FOOT FORWARD

"Marketing's job is never done. It is about perpetual motion. We must continue to innovate everyday."
> — Beth Comstock

Let's adopt some *marketing best practices* to ensure that your new marketing efforts are given the best opportunity to succeed. Putting the proper time and effort into your marketing initiatives is not enough to get what you want out of your marketing funnel. Make a list and share with your team; I call these best practices, *marketing non-negotiables.*

SPEED KILLS

Your first marketing non-negotiable is to never forget that speed kills the competition! The fastest to follow up wins more times than not. Insidesales.com published that marketing campaigns which trigger responses in less than five minutes from lead to meaningful contact experience, have a nine times greater lead conversion success rate than the competition. Automated follow up is an easy standard sales procedure to put in place that can separate you from the competition. Converting sales via speed can be accomplished with automatic lead follow up in the form of email auto-responders.

"*Always call the lead in less than five minutes of receiving the lead!*" *Speed kills the competition.* A fast call can eliminate the competition. It is a fact that you have competition and the lead decided that you might be the answer to their problem. It is your business duty to show them that they made the right choice, especially when they have other options besides you. Use speed to shut the door on the competition.

UTILIZE MULTIPLE BUSINESS PLATFORMS

Another standard practice is to *cement your business brand and marketing footprint on multiple business platforms* and seek new places to showcase your business on a monthly basis. You are purposefully growing your business' online footprint.

The world is going places and you should be there when they arrive!

FOLLOW UP

Let's dig in and build your marketing and sales transformation from a place of knowledge backed by business statistics.

- 48% of sales people never follow up with a prospect
- 25% of sales people make a second contact and stop
- 12% of sales people make more than three contacts

- 2% of sales are made on the first contact
- 3% of sales are made on the second contact
- 5% of sales are made on the third contact
- 10% of sales are made on the fourth contact
- 80% of sales are made on the fifth to twelfth contact (Source: Union Square Ventures Website)

What can we ascertain from these stats? Let's start with the easy items. You should quickly be able to see that most people are horrible with follow up. Adding strategic and purposeful follow up strategies that touch the potential customer and current customer more than five times can make a dramatic difference in the amount of sales your company closes monthly and yearly.

Potential customer follow up is one of the most under-utilized customer acquisition strategies in business today. If fact, lack of follow up with leads and current customers can erode the fabric of even the most powerful companies... and your business is no different. If it is a duck, then let's call it a duck. Most business owners, sales people, and companies are horrible with lead and customer follow up. In fact, experts say that on average a company loses 15% of its customer base each year.

If we dissect these stats correctly, we can start to reveal a customer acquisition treasure map. First, when we lump the first three stats together, then we know that 85% of our competition is no longer our competition after the third follow up with our potential customer.

- 48% of sales people never follow up with a prospect
- 25% of sales people make a second contact and stop
- 12% of sales people make more than three contacts

Compare these stats with the statistics of follow up required to actually make a sale. On average only 20% of leads are converted to customers before the fourth contact, which means that 80% of the marketplace is there for the taking without competition. Your business income treasure map has been revealed.

You have a great chance to win 80% of the business in the marketplace **IF** you follow up better than your competition. Oh, and by the way, most of your competition is already gone after the first, second, third and sometimes fourth attempt to convert a lead. You want 80% of the business? ***Then simply follow up like a champion!***

- 80% of sales are made on the fifth to twelfth contact

But, I stated earlier that most business owners are bad with the easiest part of the sales process, follow up. Why is that? Following up isn't hard. It is just a consistency plan that most businesses lack. With all that in mind, your next business non-negotiable is to *always have at least five to eight on-purpose follow up touch points with your leads*.

I'll let you off of the follow up hook for a second. Of course follow up is hard when you have 50 different hats to wear each day as a business owner. As the CEO, having to juggle everything with the business, and then adding another 50 – 100 leads/customers to keep in contact with – it is enough to drop even the most dedicated owner to their knees. But, *it is also an undeniable fact that follow up wins*, so it is a non-negotiable to find a solution to one of the greatest business income boosters: follow up!

We will tackle automation solutions in chapter eight. In the meantime, you need to start building the best follow up program you can and make it one of your largest business focuses to grow your company net worth. *Follow up, follow up, follow up is the name of the income game.*

CEO Tip: Remember we already developed our "Did you know" list and a "FAQ" list. This can be infused into your follow up procedures to stay in touch and also educate prospects towards choosing you as the right decision to be their solution.

SCOUT THE COMPETITION

"Scout The Competition! Never ever... ever... ever... ever... deploy your marketing until you scout the competition first!" – Jason Palliser

"You may have done a good job building, but your offer may still be inferior!" – Jason Palliser

One of the biggest mistakes I see business owners new and old make is to go into a marketing battle without "scouting the competition" first. The sad part about this business non-negotiable is that scouting the competition is very easy to do in today's world; yet most business owners don't add it to their standard operating procedures list as part of their marketing execution plan.

Scouting your competition should be a priority for your business and never be brushed aside if you want to become, and remain, a business force in the marketplace. I think if I paint the picture (no pun intended) for you, it may begin to sink in better. Let's just say that you are going to attack an opposing militia that is keeping you from what is rightfully yours. Let's say that you have built a surprise attack strategy to get a competitive advantage. For the sake of argument, let us also say that your plan is a good one, by most standards. Let us say that your timing is right, your body count estimations are right, and swords are your weapons of choice. BUT you decided not to use your spy to assess your competition before going into battle.

Today is the day. Your plan is in motion. You have won the element of surprise, your troops match theirs and you attack with swords drawn. Now imagine your troops with everything in place except they discover the enemy has guns drawn to defend their turf. How do you think this story ends? Let's just say, "Not well!"

The question here becomes, could this have been avoided? Of course it could have. You could have scouted the competition, you could have avoided heartache, and you could have won the battle, but you didn't. The only reason you fell short is because you did not scout the competition first to see what you were up against. The good news here is that you will not lose your life if you don't scout the business competition. But if you do not take the time to see if your marketing cannot only stand up to the competition, but also outshine the competition, then you may lose the ability to grow your business and be in danger of losing your livelihood.

Your big business non-negotiable to cement into your brand, marketing, and growth strategy is to _"Always Scout The Competition" before you deploy your customer acquisition strategies._ The bottom line here is that you need to see what the competition is offering (so your offer is better), and how they are reaching customers. Build a better plan that brings customers to you versus the competition. Remember that you are always competing for customers and marketshare, and your branding and marketing will never stop improving.

HUGE CEO RESOURCE: Depending on what type of business you are running, you can use technology to dig d-e-e-e-e-e-e-e-e-p into your competition in order to build very targeted lead capture campaigns and marketing collateral. One such mega-tool to check out your competition is _www.whatrunswhere. com_, which grabs virtually all of your competition's marketing initiatives. It can grab the competitions ads, show you where they run and sometimes it will even show you which ads are winning the most business. I'm here to teach you, give you a competitive edge, and bring value to your company. This is one advantage that can save you mountains of time in marketing trial and error, as well as save you tons of money by seeing exactly where your competition is fishing for targeted customer leads.

TWEAKING IS PEAKING! (SPLIT TEST EVERY MARKETING CAMPAIGN YOU DEPLOY!)

As we are nearing the home stretch of your marketing transformation, we want to make sure your marketing is always striving to reach its peak performance. After all, you don't want to work hard to have your business run average and experience little growth. You want it to continue to push your business to higher levels and one sure-fire way to kick start that growth is to "*Split-Test*" all of your marketing initiatives.

Split-testing your marketing can help turn ordinary marketing into extraordinary marketing. Split-testing is simply taking the hard work you've done to develop some of your best marketing campaigns and *tweaking small elements of your marketing messages and collateral to test against itself for optimal customer generation*. As an On-Purpose CEO of your business, this has to be a monster business non-negotiable that is an automatic part of your strategic business growth practice.

So, what should you do? You should start taking all of your customer lead generation practices and dissecting the messages, the offers, and the visual presentations to start making small strategic tweaks on-purpose. Look for the change that breaks open the new customer floodgates. In simpler terms, you need to make small changes to your marketing and test it against the current campaigns to see which wins and then *test it again*!

Basically, split testing is the on-purpose practice of saying, "My marketing is not good enough!" and tweaking the campaigns one piece at a time to track where you experience customer growth. This gives you real business intelligence when you track what wins and what loses. Split-testing is the smart way to constantly be improving your marketing and proactively seeking to take your business to another income level.

I suggest that you create a folder for all marketing materials, campaigns, and collateral so you can centralize the material. You may want to create a Dropbox account for it, so it is easy to share with anybody you later place in charge of improving your marketing.

Wherever you organize the collateral, the next step is to start making small changes to the marketing and placing it into the marketplace wherever you want to test the changes. The final step will be to make sure that you track everything so you can start to see the real split-testing winners from the losers. Never stop testing and your marketing will never stop improving!

SUCCESS STORY:

A client was working hard but getting marginal results from their marketing efforts. We implemented tracking to figure out what was working and what wasn't. We then split tested the efforts that weren't yielding good results, to tease out a better response. From there we implemented three new marketing activities. Presto! There was a 400% increase of quality leads within 90 days. *Success!*

Once you've implemented this strategy, here is what you get in return. You get insight into what is working and what is not. You get to see that a small change can increase your sales and business income. You get to wake up every day knowing what is making you more money, instead of guessing. You get to work on improving other areas of your business, since your split-testing is working hard to deliver you business intelligence on-purpose. You get to spend money on the right marketing initiatives, instead of the wrong ones, because your marketing is telling you what is working with data to back it up. You get to stop spending money on items that are not giving you the best growth results.

As I mentioned, one of the biggest keys here is to implement the tracking of your marketing efforts. It is not good enough to simply become a more profitable business because you are constantly testing your marketing messages; you have to attach tracking measures (*via a good CRM*) to effectively give you up-to-the-minute invaluable stats.

CONSISTENCY WINS!

Drip money from your income funnel like a champ!

Now that we have a finely tuned marketing machine in motion, it is time to juice up the lead generation engine with built-in consistency. This will be your biggest business hill to climb. I liken the consistency to a cross-country race that you are trying to win. Like a cross-country race with constant ups and downs to navigate, you need to be ready for the hills or you may lose your momentum. It should go without saying that to beat your competition to the finish line, you need to keep running smoothly.

Of course you wouldn't neglect the most vital part of your business machine, the engine. The engine in this case is your marketing consistency. *Simply put, you cannot take a break with your marketing and branding and expect to win the race.* To win more business, and repeatedly stand in the winner circle, you need a standard of marketing consistency comprised of the following practices:

- Campaigns that go out to the marketplace regularly and are not just sent when you "feel" like business is slow.
- Searching for, and deploying to new potential lead generation avenues as a monthly standard practice. (Add one new place per month to test your marketing and track the results.)
- Hit consumers every place you can with your branding and marketing. Surround them socially in order to make sure that when they are ready to buy, you are right in front of them for the sale.
- Set minimum standards to hit weekly or monthly for new customer acquisition. Visit the progress regularly in order to be nimble and make marketing adjustments on the fly.
- Never take time off from marketing your brand

and services because it is a 24-hour-a-day battle for marketshare.

The standard of consistency that keeps you collecting trophies in business starts with lead and customer follow up. Knowing what to say ahead of time, and when and how often to say it, is an invaluable part of building a customer follow up funnel that can spin income gold automatically.

CEO Resource:

Check out this link to see how I use consistency in my business:
    BiggerBusinessBlueprint.com/ContentTips

COMMIT TO A MARKETING BUDGET

Marketing wins when you commit to a plan and follow it through. We already said consistency wins every time, but in this instance I am talking about building a budget around your marketing efforts. Most business owners throw some marketing pieces together and send it out the door to see what happens. Sometimes they get results and it turns their focus to the sale, yet they forget to keep the marketing engine running.

What happens next is they finish up the sales and look around to find no more new customers are coming in the door. This is a classic mistake that most business owners make, where they take their business-eye off of the business-process to focus on the "Shiny Nickel," which is the new customer and the income it produced. Instead they need to focus on keeping the marketing funnels running smoothly to produce consistent crops of potential new customer leads.

It needs to be noted that the previously mentioned phenomena is more often than not motivated by a business owners unwillingness to spend consistent money on maintaining marketing campaign objectives to keep new customers coming in the door. This is why you, as the On-Purpose CEO of your business, need to develop a marketing budget and stick to it.

Committing to a marketing budget is the best task you can complete to get out of your own entrepreneur way and let the marketing do its job. Strategically test it every step of the way and remember that consistency wins. DO NOT fall into the habit of thinking you have enough business coming in, therefore you can make this month's numbers look even better by pulling back on the marketing expenditures. You may make your bottom line look better in the short run, but you could be costing your business positive growth for several quarters because you messed with the marketing budget.

SALES PRINCIPLES AND SECRET DATA

Time to marry our marketing with sales increasing strategies that can tip the customer scales in your favor. Your marketing is designed to gain attention and increase awareness about your products and services. Seizing the sale is the final frontier to creating your best business. Here is where I want you to really focus on *adopting non-negotiable sales practices* into your closing process. Again, the more we can build the right marketing and sales practices, the easier we can increase sales, measure the results, and grow your business income. Time to pay attention to your sales timing, sales approach, sales philosophy and sales practices. We will fine tune from the list below...

- Best times to e-mail: Between 8am – 3pm.
- Best Times to call: 4-5pm and 8-10am.
- Best Days Prospecting: Wednesday and Thursday. Tuesday is worst!

- Top Sellers commonly use LinkedIn six hours per week.
- Early Bird: 50% of sales go to the first salesperson to contact.
- Email Marketing = Two times higher ROI than cold calls, networking functions and trade shows (*Source:* Marketing Sherpa).

We've all heard the saying *timing is everything* and it can be applied to sales as well. Picking the right times to turn leads into customers can increase your sales success. For instance, if you are using e-mail, the best times to try to reach prospects is typically between 8am – 3pm for optimal results. If your sales process also involves prospect phone calls, then try to call between 4-5pm or between 8-10am to increase your sales results. This is the time that the prospects have been found to be more available and receptive to your sales efforts.

Let's add more sales formula best practices to the mix! The best days to contact prospects are Wednesday and Thursday, while generally Tuesday's are the worst for getting sales results.

CEO TIP: Take these principles and build your schedule around the best selling days and times. Fill the other days and times with non-sales activities like customer planning, offer building, FAQ creation and so on.

If the nature of your sales are more B2B (business to business), then you definitely want to submerge yourself and your sales team into www.LinkedIn.com. Take it a step further and join a strategic professional group to identify new customers. *There is income gold in the LinkedIn Groups!* Spike sales by building commonality trust in these groups and by answering questions that group members post, which can bring monster attention to your brand. (*Experts say that the top sales reps in the B2B space are spending an average of six hours per week attacking LinkedIn.*)

Connect on a much broader scale to help identify when prospects may be looking to buy a product or service that your company delivers. Basically, do your best to be right at their fingertips when they are ready to buy and you will win! Get social and get richer!

We will talk more in-depth later about the many places to generate more leads into sales, but it is important to note that *e-mail prospect engagement is producing a two times higher ROI (Return on Investment) than cold calls, networking functions, and tradeshows.* It is important to test the customer acquisition waters everywhere, but note that in most industries today e-mail touch and follow up campaigns are producing double the results versus older methods (*Source:* Marketing Sherpa).

Lastly, according to Selz.com, roughly 71% of consumers think they can get products and services cheaper online. So, what does this mean for you? It is simple. Whether you think that your products or services need to be online or not; the answer is that they do. It also strengthens the "Scout The Competition" business non-negotiable best practice, so you can see exactly what 71% of potential customers might be seeing. Build your business around beating the data you collect!

Maybe they are looking to buy your services and they saw your advertising, but statistics show that they will look online before they buy. You don't want them to find your competitors and not you, correct? Well then you better make sure that your advertising also has a clear spot for them to go online. Make sure you continue to anchor into their consumer brains that you are the right choice.

A PICTURE IS WORTH...

Beefing up your _visual depiction of your products and services_ can help cement your brand and offerings up to 60 times more than just plain text marketing initiatives alone. Time to _spice up your ads with better graphics_ and track the lead conversion and sales increase by tweaking your marketing. Paint a better picture to stand out and be more memorable to your prospects. As previously stated, you are 63 times more memorable when your offerings have great graphics that lead into a story versus a simple stat-based marketing style. And, when the story helps paint the problem clearly to resonate with the prospects struggles, you are increasing your chances of striking prospect-to-customer gold.

NURTURE AND TRACK

Let's see where we can put some standard sales practices in place that help you stand out from the rest. It has been estimated that roughly 65% of all business owners do not have any lead nurturing campaigns in place to grab, let alone keep, current customers coming back for more.

Dive even deeper into the opportunity to be better than the competition; it also should be noted that out of the roughly 35% of businesses that _do_ have a nurturing campaign in place, a whopping 79% of them do not have any way to track the results and trends of their campaigns. They are left to guess what is working or not working. Remember, they are trying to take business away from you every day, but without tracking a deliberate on-purpose planning and tracking, they are simply growing by accident and probably losing money by focusing on the wrong critical business growth and sales initiatives.

Can you see the clear opportunity here? _Devoting valuable_ _business time to putting your best follow up campaigns/nurturing_ _campaigns in place, coupled with tracking, can send your sales_ _and business opportunities into the Entrepreneur Stratosphere!_

We are in the 21st century and your business growth and survival depends on how effectively you can track, test and automate your business growth strategies.

You need to fast track deciding what CRM tool you are going to put in place to run and track your campaigns effectively. Your modern business-life depends on it.

Pay Attention Here! We are not trading chickens for milk here! No matter what you are selling, what you are trading, what products or services you're offering, the business that tracks the entire process the best, can and will win in today's marketplace!

Nurture and follow up better! Add the best tracking component you can find and begin to make the better business decisions by intelligent default. Get this done and become an unparalleled business competitor in today's marketplace.

Setting aside the intelligence the tracking will deliver for a minute, just being better than your competition with nurturing alone, can get you a 10% - 20% increase in customer sales. How would an extra 10% to 20% in sales help your business look? I am guessing, pretty good!

BUSINESS DEVELOPMENT BEST PRACTICES

On the journey to be the best modern business owner you can be, there are a few more staples that earmark a successful modern business. One point of emphasis to get more customers and keep them should be to understand that your ability to close and keep customers is, "_Only as good as your best point of_ *customer contact!"*

Simply put, the consumer is comfortable with the relationship they have created with someone in your organization. Work hard to maintain the connection by either keeping consistency with one point of contact, or if that is logistically tough to accomplish, then make certain that your current point of contact documents everything about the consumer and details the relationship they have with them. If the consumer has to be passed to someone else, then the transition is smoother everything about the consumer is documented for greater insight on how to serve him or her well.

Document, document, document the process well! What process?
Any Process! Every Process!

> *You* are in the 21st century and this means it is easier than ever to develop consistent sales practices for your team and future team as you grow. An On-Purpose CEO business to-do item is to *shoot videos on how you want your team to be trained to sell.*

Process documenting and video documenting business practices gives you two leverage items. First, it ***helps develop sales consistency*** for when it comes time to train more sales staff. Second, by having videos in place to train independent of your valuable CEO time, it ***removes you from the training equation***.

> **CEO RESOURCE:** A resource you may want to use to help with this is *www.jingproject.com*, which allows for video creation right on your computer screen for up to five minutes. *Cool Feature:* It automatically e-mails you the video link when you are done, so you can share instantly!

SALES TECHNIQUES

We all know that things change, so why wouldn't consumer sales approaches and interactions change as well? The answer is: they should and do. Today's consumer is different so the way you interact and sell has evolved as well.

Today's more sophisticated consumer responds well to the _Doctor Approach to Sales_ versus normal selling. (Older sales approaches are more interrupt, pitch, and close style-based.) Today's consumer has way more information at their fingertips, and sales techniques have adapted for a softer approach like a doctor-patient based relationship, where you listen, diagnose and then prescribe. This can help increase sales according to Mark Roberge – Hubspot.com.

Another sales increasing technique that is effective today, is the practice of _surrounding your perfect customer socially_ so no matter where they turn, they find themselves submerged in your products and services, which gently pushes their buying triggers towards buying from you. You have to surround your future customers socially, which is why a big portion of your business efforts are to understand the mind of your perfect customer. Know where they swim and start swimming with them in order to build a social bubble around them. (_Source:_ Jill Rowley – Oracle)

The smartphone has put a high-speed information super engine in every one of your future customer's hands and you have to engage and surround them instantly to secure more sales opportunities. If you want to win the customer acquisition battle, then speed is the number one sales weapon to swing. Be everywhere with your brand and - even more important - be everywhere your perfect customer lives and breaths online. This includes all of the normal social media staples like Facebook, but also means joining specialized groups your customer "likes" on sites like LinkedIn.com.

Fill in your time-blocked appointments with the priority items in the order you've ranked them. Document like a monster all along the way. It will save you hundreds of hours later.

Below are some business-growth calendar considerations (Create a separate word document for each):

- Set up an account with www.jingproject.com to start shooting screen capture tutorials from your computer. (Mini-Goal: Shoot two or three videos to use to train others.)
- Perfect Customer Persona Development
- Unique Selling Proposition Development
- Logo Creation
- Tag Line Creation
- Sales Practices
- Fine tune your FAQs and your top ten Did You Knows.
- Turn the FAQs and top ten into e-mails.
- Add the FAQs and top ten to your website.
- Research CRM Tools to choose one to run your automated show forever.
- Competitor Research
- Scout the competition. (www.whatrunswhere.com)
- Create follow up practices.
- Add re-occurring calendar reminders to always be split-testing.
- Develop your best prospect follow up campaigns 7-12 touch-points deep! (e-mails and call procedures)
- Create a "Marketing Folder or Word Doc" to store good creative headlines and marketing messages from competitor research to use later.
- Develop a customer survey to find out how to serve your customers even better.
- Seek out the right person to help you graphically show your product offerings and make memorable marketing.

- Share the sale stats with your team. Print and display them. Consistency Wins! (Show everyone)
- Test out your CRM tracking. Set weekly reminders to review your marketing stats to help you tweak your sales hooks and marketing with business intelligence.
- Develop a marketing budget and stick to it.
- Use the "Secret Sales Data" info to block out your calendar to call on the right days and times. Do the same for e-mail. (SUPER EASY TO DO. THIS IS A TWO MINUTE ACTIVITY) – Your reward is a calendar filled with marketing and sales opportunity optimizers that put you on a customer closing mission!
- Spend time typing out a "Hiring Practices Blueprint" and share with the right people.

One-by-one these items will get accomplished and you can start to experience a modern business that grows purposefully and runs at levels that you previously thought were not possible without a giant workforce. You can look like a business giant, profit like a business giant, and do it all without the giant price tag if you let the systems and tools of today's world run the show for you.

You command and the tools will execute your every business wish. You are well on your way to becoming a more profitable business machine that is marching towards running without you as the engine. That equals your most prized business possession.... Leverage!

"To Grow You Need To Get Out Of Your Own Way!"
–Jason Palliser

Now take a breather and go fishing or do whatever it is that makes you happy. You deserve it.

CEO RESOURCE: Not sure how your marketing is doing?
Request a Marketing Critique:
BiggerBusinessBlueprint.com/MktingReview

Chapter 7:

Lead Generation Jungle!

TIME TO HUNT, ATTRACT, ENGAGE AND CAPTURE THE CUSTOMER PRIZE!

Lead Generation is the first step to growing your business opportunities. Technology has turned the lead generation process into a seemingly endless expedition. Even the most skilled business hunter would be smart to explore new territories to uncover new opportunities for capture.

Imagine you are a lion looking for food (new customers) and you have an endless jungle to hunt in. Now imagine you are hunting where all of the other lions are hunting. Doesn't it make sense that it will be harder to survive unless you are a better hunter than your competition? Of course it makes sense. So, there are two things you can do to help increase your chances of survival in the lead generation jungle. First is to become a better hunter than your competition. Second is to find new places to hunt with less competition to help secure your crown as the king of the business-jungle.

In this chapter we will look to explore the vast lead generation landscape to help uncover customer opportunities and let your marketing campaigns serve as the bait to capture your new customer base. After all, we have already established that in business today, it is a jungle out there and the competition is ready to strike. *Time to hunt or be the hunted.*

WELCOME TO THE JUNGLE...
[ONLINE AND OFFLINE MARKETING]

When it comes to navigating the landscape of lead generation today, it literally is a jungle out there. The good news is that there are so many places to hunt for new customers that the possibilities are endless. The bad news is that there are so many places that most business owners do not know where to start or what to do. With so many places to hunt it can be confusing and dangerous.

Discovering your new customer potential starts with exploring the online and offline lead generation jungle and the benefits of each. Find your best places to hunt and develop your best plan in these different areas to not only survive, but thrive over the competition.

HUNTING ONLINE [ADVANTAGES]

Hunting online for new customers has some very distinct advantages. The obvious one is that online advertising is typically much more cost effective. You can do it from your couch, which is why I call <u>online marketing</u>, *"The no gas money spent program!"* That bleeds into the second big advantage of online customer hunting, saving time by reaching customers online. The third advantage is that you are officially open globally, 24/7, which is definitely the sign of a 21st century business. The fourth advantage is that your profit margins can skyrocket by automating some or all of your process (versus having to delegate to others, which lowers profit margins).

Most CEOs may not know this game changer yet, but <u>*you can sniper hunt for customers versus the shotgun approach*</u>. Online venues allow you (to an extent) to zero-in on your perfect customer persona with pinpoint accuracy using criteria such as age, gender, location, interests and more. Spreading marketing everywhere with no real direction can cost a ton of money and deliver few results. The ability to sniper hunt for customers is a victory.

<u>*Example: Strategically join groups on various social sites centered on your expertise or that your offerings are a definite solution for. With the Internet and search bars you can sniper hunt for customers*</u>! You don't have to guess what groups are about, they are labeled for your viewing and hunting pleasure, which streamlines your customer acquisition attack!

A huge benefit to hunting online for customers is that data collection can be hands-free if you've set up your tracking CRM system already and it automatically categorizes the prospects for you. This is what I call an unfair hunting advantage! There are many more reasons, but these should be more than enough motivation to have you licking your business chops. Let's explore some online hunting grounds to capture more customer prey!

ONLINE HUNTING GROUNDS...

There are tons of places to choose from to digitally grow your business and brand. It could be a whole separate book. I am going to briefly touch upon a few ways to work your business online and help lay the foundation to build your online strategy.

EMAIL

The logical first choice is grabbing customers from your _e-mail_ list of prospects and clients. We have already put together the marketing top ten's to send out and e-mail is the easiest way to get your opportunities flowing. I already discussed that email marketing has produced two times greater ROI than other traditional methods, so organize your contacts and market to each target category according to their perfect customer persona. This is free to do, so build out a monster nurture/follow up campaign and start seizing opportunities. Use your "Did You Knows" and "FAQs" that you created back in chapter four to _engage them_. Through engagement you will get the sale, the repeat sale, and the referrals.

TEXT MESSAGE

The next online lead generation and customer engagement model to address is text messaging. It is a fact that everyone looks at his or her texts. Knowing that, why would you not look to capitalize on that with offers? You can send texts that say anything you want and you KNOW they will check their text messages. It is as closes as you can get to guaranteed delivery and exposure! Make a point to test this out to see the engagement.

(Text Example: You text and thank them for their business and also say "As a show of our appreciation, click here www.XYZ. com and see exclusive discounts we've complied just for you. We value your business!") Not hard at all! Steal this verbiage if you want to... my gift to you!

126

Taking text message engagement and sales even further, you may want to put a service like www.SendHub.com on your to-do list of resources to check out. They will allow you to send mass text messages all at once to reach a broad audience. Uh... like... to all of your contacts, customers, and prospects at once! This can bring a huge spike of current and potential customer traffic to your business initiatives.

ATTACKING THE BIGGEST ONLINE JUNGLE OF ALL... SOCIAL MEDIA SITES!

Social media is here to stay. To hunt in this jungle we need to lay some _online social business non-negotiables_ for you. You have to set up your business page or pages on Facebook and Google+. Set up your Twitter account for your business brand as well. You can have thousands connect with you and your products and services virtually overnight with Twitter and their easy one-click follow system.

Some social platforms to look into for customer acquisitions are the following:

- Facebook
- Twitter
- LinkedIn
- Digg
- Google+
- StumbleUpon
- Tumblr
- Instagram
- Reddit
- Backpage

Tapping into these social platforms not only helps bring in more business and more exposure, it also helps with the various search engine rankings. Your business is earmarked on these _Authority Websites_, which gives you better online search rankings when people search for products and services in your niche. Future customers start organically find you as a result.

Block your calendar to set up accounts on these sites and start to rise in the search engines and gain more marketshare. They are authority sites because they have millions, if not billions of visitors a month. It carries tremendous weight for your online presence when you've anchored your business on the various sites listed in this chapter.

> **CEO Tip:** 84% of online buyers refer to at least one social media site for recommendations before buying. (*Source:* Selz.com)

Special Promise: *Don't worry! I promise in the next chapter on leverage that we can help you get this done fast, cheap, and easy.*

SOCIAL MEDIA GROUPS

Let's attack a couple of specific ones. Spend smart business time on sites like www.LinkedIn.com and www.Meetup.com to get familiar with them and learn how it can explode your business opportunity. *The key on these wonderful customer-generating sites is to strategically join the right groups.* This is hands-down where I have brought in the most customers and made the most money for my various businesses. The strategic groups are sales and income gold.

Why, you might ask? Because they let you use their search functions to find *groups that align perfectly with your product and service offerings*. The beauty here is in the technology. The groups compile discussions that are centered on your business niche solutions. These discussions are then well-organized and delivered in a "Daily Digest" format to your normal e-mail inbox every day. You read that correctly! The sites organize the previous day's discussions into one daily e-mail for you to click and answer like a solutions-ninja! If you are in the right groups, you can get daily discussions around your niche. From there it is simple to connect with potential new customers and solve their problems with your products and services.

Wait a minute! Slow down to digest this. *You can join groups strategically, go about your normal business day, and wake up in the morning with an e-mail listing all discussions in your strategic groups. You can click the discussions where you can provide a solution and strike deals from you couch!*

If you **love this section**, then please let your fellow entrepreneurs know by going to Twitter or Facebook and posting a message using **#BiggerBusinessBlueprint** so we can all share in your enthusiasm.

> **CEO To-Do Item and Non-Negotiable:** Join groups on LinkedIn.com and Meetup.com and ALWAYS open the discussion group e-mails first every day! They may be raising their hand to buy from you!

CRAIGSLIST

The next section of the online jungle to explore is CraigsList.org. At last check it was ranked as the sixth website in America and boasts roughly 111,000,000 visitors a month. I'm pretty sure that some of them are your future customers and clients. People are buying and selling virtually everything under the sun on www.CraigsList.org, so you need to get familiar with how to "Post an Ad" and also search the "Want Ads" section of the website to grab a seemingly endless amount of potential customer and potential sales opportunity.

You can use CraigsList to hire people to promote your brand, products, and services as well. Offer them a commission for bringing you qualified leads that turn into sales. By the way, you can do this from the couch right now in less than two minutes if you want more business!

IF THIS, THEN THAT (RECIPES FOR SUCCESS!)

Instead of trolling websites like this all day, wouldn't you like to get an e-mail or text message the exact moment someone wants your business solution? Of course you would! _We might need to take a break so you can go shower_ because using Ifttt.com is one of the dirtiest weapons I utilize to help business owners move their income needle due north. That is correct! The customers are automatically coming to you! Set up triggering events to notify you when new opportunities are posted online! When consulting, I set up recipes for my consulting clients and let the lead opportunities roll in. Set up some IFTTT.com recipes.

(You can also automate the lead funnel directly into your business lap. _As a monster automation income blast tip, I strongly suggest you go to www.ifttt.com and set up some CraigsList recipe triggers_. If done correctly, you may be the first human to know when someone is looking for your exact business offering and if we refer back to our sales/marketing chapter, I'm pretty sure we said the early bird get the worm. The first to the customer usually wins.

> CEO RESOURCE: **_www.ifttt.com_** (Automated Recipes)

GETTING TO KNOW YOU...

You can also grow your brand by using online weapons to let the consumer world get to know you better. What do I mean and how do we do that? _It is a fact that people do business with people they feel like they know and they like_. That being said, the best way to start to drop anchor and fish for schools of customers is to activate your www.YouTube.com account and add video to your brand. Oh, and by the way, YouTube is a monster authority website (ranked third in the world) and is owned by the first website in the world, Google! _Have your brand and offerings come to life with video_. It is no secret that _everyone_ loves video, so use it to your business advantage.

Start shooting videos about your business, your products, your offerings, helpful tips and everything else in between. Consumers love video! Product sales today are more about trust than ever and there is no better way to start building trust than connecting with people via video. The power of video can explode your business. Why? Because video can convey emotion and feeling way better than written marketing copy ever can! You are connecting your products and services to your customers in a more personal way. The prospects get to know you and your company on a deeper level and these connections can turn into loads of cash.

You want a monster business? You want to blow through all of your income goals? Get on the video bandwagon as soon as possible. Hire video specialists if you need to off of websites like www.fiverr.com, where there are video ninjas to help you for as little as five dollars. You can also increase your business exposure by using tools like www.tubetoolbox.com to automatically connect you with your target customers and get hundreds, if not thousands of views that help your business take off.

Remember: _Don't worry! I've got you covered on the help you may want or need in the chapter on "Leverage," so let's keep rolling!_

Things you can and should video:

- Welcome video to your business. They get to know you 100x easier!
- FAQs video. Remember, getting to know you equals an increase in sales.
- "How To" videos on anything that helps them as a value-add. Ex: Dry Cleaner – Shoot a short video on the top three ways to keep your shirts looking new!
- Mission statement video!
- Testimonials!

Add these videos to your website, add the links to the videos in your e-mail follow up campaigns, and send them out to your social media outlets. It is easy! All you have to do is copy and paste.

> **CEO BIZ NON-NEGOTIABLE:** Always put a link to your website or your lead capture pages in the description box of your YouTube videos.

PAY PER CLICK ADS

Use Pay-Per-Click Ads to reach new customers. This is a strategy you can use on multiple websites that allow for advertising opportunities. Some examples are Google, Facebook, Backpage, Plenty Of Fish (Dating Website), and many more. The concept is easy. You create a catchy ad that can be placed on these sites. You may get tons of exposure and thousands of pairs of eyeballs looking at your ads, but you don't really pay anything unless they click on your ad. Remember, most of these sites let you drill down to "highly targeted" perfect customer opportunities.

Essentially, you can use this strategy to shoot fish in a barrel.

For instance, let's say you sell guitars and you want to sell Facebook users guitars in the St. Louis area. You could look to place a Pay-Per-Click Ad on Facebook and select the following: Only show to people in St. Louis, with musical interests, and between the ages of X and Y. Then only those people will see your ad. Chances are if they click, that your opportunity to sell a guitar is multiplied by a large percentage. Target marketing in this fashion rocks and can soar your profitability. Remember, sniper approach versus shotgun approach.

One final wrinkle to add on this subject is that some sites will also allow you to show ads to your custom audience. You can upload contact e-mails for prospect and/or past customers and exclusively place ads in front of them. Imagine doing this and they keep seeing you and your brand pop up, but you are not paying unless they click. Two big things are happening here. One is that this approach is anchoring your brand in their minds. Two is that when you do actually have to pay for a click, you know it is the right lead clicking and the minimal cost is well worth it's weight in gold. Why? Because they have contacted you before, or bought from you before, and you know they are your perfect audience. I hope that you are becoming a fan of this type of advertising to grow your brand like a 21st century champ.

PRESS RELEASES

The last item I will explore with you to help navigate the jungle better together is the art of using _Press Releases_ to get some exposure for you and your brand. You read me correct! Your business can experience a tidal wave of exposure via press releases. Let's break this down together. A press release is simply no more than a 500-700 word article that typically takes a current newsworthy subject and weaves your product or services into the issue. Since it is online we can add a couple of links to places that lead the reader to your "calls to action" and get them to become your customer!

Let me let you off of the hook here. Your first thought was probably, "Great Jason, I am not a writer and have no clue where to start!" Fair enough. But what you may not know is that there are services that will write the press release for you for as little as $7-$12. Hire them on places like www.textbroker.com, where professional writers can do this for you in their sleep.

Press Release Tutorial Video:

https://youtu.be/9S5BdxENSpU

Warning... this guy is boring, but it will give you an understanding of how press releases can give you massive exposure.

Once the press release is written, then it is ready for services to distribute your message to the media, like www.prlog.org for free press releases and www.prweb.com for paid ones. Utilize these press releases for either SEO purposes or for lead capture purposes. If your goal is to get better search engine rankings, then add a couple of links in the press release to your website. If your goal is to get more leads to close, then add lead capture links into your press release and do not link your generic website in them.

For a drop in the bucket, you may literally be picked up by online publications like Yahoo.com, CNN.com, ABC.com, MSNBC.com and more. This can mean thousands upon thousands of consumers reading your message. Please try to keep this our Ninja Marketing and Branding Secret!

ONLINE GROWTH PLANNING TIPS...

Here are some online planning tips as you get ready to embark on this online business growth journey. Utilize some of these methods to push your projects and initiatives forward. Before you dive in though, remember to document, document, document in order to easily delegate later for leverage.

(Centralize your social media collateral via Word Document: passwords, websites, your posting practices, marketing collateral and so on…)

TUTORIALS

Use YouTube.com as a massive "How to" weapon for anything you need to learn as it relates to your online business growth plan. The reason YouTube.com is my favorite site is because you can search for anything you need help with. There is a video with a step-by-step process already created that you can start, stop, and execute at your own pace to accomplish every business strategy you can imagine. This means you have a 24-hour a day helper at your fingertips, so use it to your advantage. For instance, you can YouTube search the following:

- How to create a Facebook Business Page?
- How to grow my Twitter presence?
- How to market on CraigsList?
- Social Media Best Practices
- And anything else you can think of….

SYNDICATION TOOLS

The cool (and possibly overwhelming) part about the massive opportunity of being virtually everywhere online is that you *have* to be everywhere online. I strongly suggest using "Syndication Tools" such as www.hootsuite.com to help get your marketing and branding to multiple sites at once. Essentially, place your marketing on Hootsuite.com and it will deliver everywhere - saving you valuable business time for other growth strategies.

Another syndication tool to utilize is "If this, Then That!" or www.ifttt.com to grab customers or push out offers to multiple places via "Recipes" that you can create. Check it out. You will be blown away from the seemingly endless possibilities. The triggers you set up can deliver opportunity right to you!

BRING IN HELP

As the On-Purpose CEO of your company, hopefully your plan is to experience exponential growth through these methods. At some point hopefully you raise your hand for help and bring on experts with online marketing and brand development to run the income boost plan for you. Places you can go for help are Upwork.com and Fiverr.com to help with all of these strategies.

My hope for you is that after reading this book, you create a tidal wave of new business and become the king of the online jungle. Even the king of the jungle needs help! I suggest you eventually look to hire an online brand manager to keep your business bellowing a ground-shaking roar that invokes fear in all of your competitors in the online marketplace.

ONLINE NON-NEGOTIABLES

There are a few non-negotiable online items and initiatives that you need to make sure you have in place as you embark on becoming the king of the online jungle. Make these a priority and devote time on your business calendar to get these in motion.

DIRECTORIES

One non-negotiable is to _get your company or companies listed in as many of the online directories as you can_, so when consumers search they can find you 100x easier. Places like Google, Bing, Yahoo, Yelp, Yp.com, Yellowbook, Local.com, Angie's List, Foursquare, and many more. There are places that will do this for you for peanuts like www.knowem.com. This can give your brand a very nice boost to place you in front of consumers faster than your competition, which can translate into more income for you.

CONTACT INFORMATION

An easy non-negotiable is to _make sure that you have strong and very clear profile information embedded into your online profiles_. Make sure that it has your website link, contact information, and a good explanation of what your company does and offers. If you have this non-negotiable done, then as consumers go through their buying cycle, it is easy to see that you are a potential solution and it is easy to do business with you. What a novel idea, huh? You may smile, but I've seen tons of business owners over my years of teaching that have profiles that say something similar to "I can replace your roof" and nothing else. Guess it is time to go on a "business owner Easter-Egg hunt" to find their contact details!

> **CEO NON-NEGOTIABLE:** Make it EASY to do business with you!

A closely related non-negotiable is to _make sure that you build good marketing/brand building business pages on websites_ like Facebook, which let you add business pages to showcase your value/offerings. Facebook makes it so easy that you can set one up in less than two minutes. You can always super-size it later, but at the very least you should get one set up with your product and service offerings on it (and contact details).

WEBSITE

Setting up your business website is an absolute business non-negotiable! You have to set it up because it is your "24/7 Open For Business" sign that lets the world know (if done correctly) everything that your company embodies and has to offer.

For some of you reading this, it may make your heart start beating differently because you think with a non-21st century brain that tells you building, let alone managing a business website is light-years past your ability. Here is the dirty little website secret. They are mega easy to set up and just as easy to manage. If you can type words and hit a save button, then you can manage your website just as easy as creating and saving a word document.

Think I'm joking? Okay, go visit www.templatemonster.com and see how many styles there are to choose from for your website's look and feel. See how cheap it is. After you buy a template you like, you can have someone attach it to the domain name you bought for your company off of a place like www.godaddy.com. For as little as $100 - $600 you can have a beautiful website to show the world.

Websites are a collection of pages and articles. Here's a list of what to add to your website: (If you are starting from scratch, pace yourself. You can go live with one page and add overtime.)

- Contact Us Page
- Services Offered Page
- About Us Page – Strong Profile and Clear Contact Info.
- Mission Statement Page

- Testimonial Page
- Lead Capture Pages
- Depending on the business type: Purchase Links
- Strong Home Page – Paint The Picture and Tell The Story
- Product Pages
- Depending on the business: Before and After Pages w/ photos/verbiage
- FAQ page
- Top 10 Page (Did you knows)

CEO RESOURCE: Website Creation The Right Way: (Web site building services & platform optimized) BiggerBusinessBlueprint.com/WebHelp

---

TRACKING

Finally, we need to _make sure you set up "Lead Capture" pages_ to grab prospects because they searched, found you, and your marketing piqued their interest. We will go more into this when we talk about leverage, but we need to activate a business CRM (customer relationship management) tool that allows you to create, track and tweak lead capture pages, in order for you to close sales and grab new customers hands-free while you sleep or vacation. Pause… and insert vacation palm trees in your mind, please.

CEO ACTIVITY: Online Initiative Task Scheduling

- Take ten minutes to place six separate one-hour appointments on your calendar to accomplish some of the online business growth initiatives in this chapter.

CEO RESOURCE: Customized Online Marketing
Game Plan:
 BiggerBusinessBlueprint.com/OnlineMkting

OFFLINE HUNTING GROUNDS AND RESOURCES

To be a modern business, you need to meet the consumer world where they live and breathe, which is online. To be a modern business that is a force to be reckoned with, you need to *dominate the offline marketing jungle* as well. This section may be more familiar to you, but we are going to expand our hunt for the perfect customers in some offline areas that you more than likely have never explored before.

The goal is to develop some offline strategies that can produce even greater business income by widening our lead generation net to capture customers. It is important to note that depending on what type of business you are in, or looking to build wealth in, that some of these strategies may not apply.

Regardless, I would pay special attention to the process and intent behind these offline strategies. They can be the foundation for a potential tweak to your approach or approaches that unlocks more revenue than what you have today.

The offline strategies are a little more straightforward; therefore I will be a little more direct with the explanation and/or execution plans. Remember, before the advent of the Internet, pretty much all marketing for business owners was offline. Billions have been made with offline marketing and branding techniques to grow a business. Your business is no different. Time to tackle a few of these together and further establish your business as the King of the Business Jungle.

PRINT MEDIA

I will start with the usual offline marketing suspects that we are most familiar with, like *local publications and newspapers*. These are some of the most popular offline strategies that business owners use for customer acquisition. Local publications can be weekly mini-papers or booklets, much like the "Thrifty Nickel" in my home city of St. Louis. There are also traditional newspaper publications where you can place ads for customer acquisition.

Please take note and consider that the cost for advertising here is much cheaper than you may think with the advent of digital media. You can get great exposure for cheap via local publications and newspapers.

You can market in college papers. This is very useful for selling your stuff to a younger demographic. Also, it is relatively inexpensive to advertise here. Your competition probably isn't swimming here, so wouldn't you like to fish alone and catch the most fish? Of course you would. Make a to-do item to grab a college newspaper in the next seven to ten days and take a peek at what is being offered (scouting).

CEO ACTIVITY: Call two publications next week and see what it costs to runs some marketing ads with them. Then place an ad!

> **CEO Tip:** Consider the print audience here, which is typically an older audience. If your offerings are more suited for this type of audience, then places some ads ASAP! Lastly, consider that this audience is still doing things the old fashioned way, which you can use to your advantage if you choose to hunt here. What I mean is that this type of potential customer profile, which still reads physical publications, is a type that is consistent and if you market to them here correctly, you can grab a very loyal customer. (Hmm... You see where I'm going here?) Use this knowledge to your advantage when building your marketing hooks.
>
> Example: If you are a restaurant owner, then hit them with "Blue Light Special Ads" and gain a _Steady Eddie_ loyal customer that comes to eat with you every Tuesday and Friday.

MAIL

DIRECT MAIL

Our next offline marketing strategy involves utilizing direct mail. One of the biggest offline forms of lead generation is direct mail marketing using letters and postcards. I previously mentioned exploring new territories of the jungle to hunt and direct mail is definitely one on those areas. With direct mail, what I typically hear is that most of my trainees and/or clients simply don't know where to start. So, let me build out the simple plan to reaching new customers through direct mail efforts.

The first step is locating names and addresses of prospects you want to mail to. There are a few places I would recommend starting with to locate targeted lists of potential customers. (www.listability.com and www.melissadata.com and for real estate specific data www.listsource.com)

Each website offers the opportunity to buy a targeted or specialized list of names and addresses to mail to for lead generation. The demographic possibilities are seemingly endless. As an example, right from the home page on Listability. com, you can click on specialty lists and choose lists for new business owners, medical professionals, charitable donors, pet owners, women business owners, corporate headquarters, intergenerational family lists and many more. Do you see why this may be customer acquisition gold for you? Instead of aimlessly throwing out marketing everywhere, you can be very targeted and know you are hitting your customer's sweet spot by buying targeted lists.

From here it is time to mail out to the names and addresses that were electronically sent to you. You can look up "mail houses" that can send the marketing out in bulk for you, or do it yourself.

Before you hit *go* on your direct mail campaigns, there is one big note and one giant business tip for you so you can put your best business-foot forward. It should be noted that you typically get a one to three percent response rate from mailings. Secondly, for the best response rates, I would mail to each address five times or more. After all, you've already bought the list, so you don't have to buy it again. Consistency wins! Remember, you are fishing where most don't fish, so there is less competition for you to win customers.

MAILING COUPONS

A close cousin to direct mail is to participate in coupon packs. So rather than mail out a letter or postcard to every address on your list, partner with other local businesses to send packages of coupons. Coupon packs have a lower cost than direct mail campaigns because the print and mailing costs are split between the participating businesses. Coupon packs also have a higher open rate, so if your business is conducive to coupons, spend sometime investigating this option.

EVENTS

Attending, sponsoring, or speaking at events is a great way to make an impression about your business. By allowing prospective clients to see you and get to know you as a brand ambassador, they will associate your company with good things. The visibility and authority of sponsoring or speaking can catapult your company into a growth cycle. Take a look at these suggestions to get out and mingle.

TRADESHOWS AND CONVENTIONS

After reading this paragraph, I want you to take a two-minute break. Why? Because I want you to search for *"Trade Shows or Conventions."* Find ones in your business wheelhouse and search for requirements to become a vendor. This is beautiful offline face-to-face marketing. At the very least, put them on your calendar to go and scout the competition, because they are attending and you should be too. Don't let them out-market you! Search, e-mail, or call about vendor options and execute. Your net worth will thank you!

NETWORKING GROUPS

If you are more B2B sales, then joining the chamber of commerce can definitely give your business and income a boost. The chamber is a collection of local business and meets once or twice a month for mixers.

You may also want to try joining a _BNI Group_. This is where you meet with other business professionals in a planned meeting session on a weekly basis. You share referrals to help each other grow their respective businesses. There is a pretty rigid time commitment for BNI and if you go rogue by not showing up, you may be ousted from the group. Be aware and follow the rules.

Sponsor

You can try to _sponsor local sports tournaments_ to get more exposure. Before you commit to this, ask what type of exposure you'll get. Seek out sponsorships that allow you to put up signage or even give you a chance to speak to the masses. Same thing goes for _sponsoring local fairs, county fairs, church fairs_ and so on. Also know that sometimes these events don't cost you money, but rather time, because they may just want your help serving the patrons. Exposure, exposure, exposure! Charity events are a great place to network while in the spirit of giving, and can bring in tons of business. Give and get in return is a great way to grow the business.

Again, if I were you, I would make a business to-do list that includes "sponsoring two local events or causes within the next six months." Once you mentally commit and put it in writing, the chances of you executing the business-building task go up tenfold!

Public Speaking

Building your company's offline style can also be accomplished by _seeking out meetings and venues to speak at about your area of expertise_. This is a monster way to get some massive brand awareness out about your company. I know that it does not come naturally for some of you, but just realize it does not have to be the state of the union. It just has to be good and relevant information.

Hint: You might want to build a press release about you and your company first, so you can forward it to potential speaking opportunities.

SIGNAGE

BANDIT SIGNS

Capture business with bandit signs. You know, those little 1.5-foot by 2-foot signs at every stop sign/light and every exit ramp? Bandit signs are a great way to capture the attention of local traffic and get new customers. This is very cheap marketing and it can get you great results, depending on what your business offers, of course.

You can put a short and sweet message on them to motivate potential customers to call or visit your website. Part of the reason they get results is that people are caged animals in their cars, so there is nothing better to do than to glance around and see what you find. Please note that they get taken down a lot, so don't be upset as they disappear over time.

You can grab them from places like www.dirtcheapsigns.com or www.banditsigns.com. Then you can hire someone to put them out for you as well. Just put an ad on CraigsList and you are done. I suggest that you have the person send you pictures of the signs they put out for you, so you know it is done.

Example: I was driving to work and off the exit ramp there was a bandit sign that said, "I'll clean your carpets for you while you work. Super Cheap," and then it had the number. I called it from the light and talked to him and before I showed up at work, I had scheduled a carpet cleaning for the next day.

Because he paid roughly $250 or less to get 100 bandit signs, he captured me as a client and he got three more referrals from me as well. Hmm… money well spent? I think so!

You have competition; so don't let them steal your customers because of simple offline marketing tactics that you have not tried yet. Your cleaning service may be superior to his. Your price may be better. But you cannot win if he markets better than you and gets to the customers first.

BILLBOARDS

A bigger offline marketing item to check into is to *investigate using billboard marketing*. I'm not saying that you are going to do it, but I am saying that if you want to become the best business owner you can be, block out time to check into the cost of billboard advertising. It may be cheaper than you think. Also, in the age of digital marketing, you can potentially advertise on a digital billboard much cheaper than you think. Capture loads of new business as people connect with you on their way to and from work.

BUS STOPS AND MASS TRANSPORTATION

Along the line of billboards, bus stops, buses, and interior bus advertising are all possibilities. Same thing goes for subways and other forms of mass transportation. If you are marketing to college students, or in major cities, this is a key spot to get your word out. Check out rates for interior or exterior signage. **Hint:** interior signs have a captive audience.

FLYERS

Don't forget the power of the flyer. Hand 'em out. Post 'em. Put 'em on cars, walls, etc. They get taken down fairly quickly, but they also leave a quick impression for very little output of time and energy. You can even hire someone to do the work, just ask them to take a picture when they're done to prove they deserve their paycheck.

> **CEO NON-NEGOTIABLE:** I will NOT be out-marketed! Ever!

BROADCAST MEDIA

You'd be surprised by the affordability of _TV and Radio advertising._ With the advent of the Internet, the costs have gone down significantly. Block out an hour and call three radio and three TV stations and ask them what it costs to advertise with them. You _NEED_ to know your options! By the way, when you execute this task, you will find they have whole departments that are designed to target the right times and spots for you to advertise based on your target audience. They have mega-valuable demographic information ready for you to maximize your exposure to the right audience. You won't know until you plan it out and call. No more winking in the dark! Explore all of your options my business-ninja!

BRANDED COLLATERAL

You can _use branded items to spread your company name and offerings._ You can use fridge magnets and t-shirts. These are cheap ways to get constant branding of your company in the marketplace. Pens and wearable collateral work well because it can be viewed and passed on.

A little bonus note for you as well. You can make extra money on the t-shirt idea by using services like www.teespring.com, which allows you to create a t-shirt right on their site (maybe because you thought of something really smart, funny, or catchy) and it can immediately be available for sale. You get a piece of the action without all of the other headache stuff involved. Another quick note! I want you to turn your kids into entrepreneurs as well, so send them here and they could be making money as well.

BUSINESS CARDS

Yes! Good old-fashioned business cards are still a valid way to gain business. Any good business owner should never leave home without them! Just have them in your glove box, your laptop bag, your office, your home, and anywhere else you may be that might command a business conversation. Ask to leave some at your dry cleaner. You've seen them there when you drop off your clothes, so why are your cards not there as well? *Please don't answer that in your mind!* No matter what your answer is, I will go out on a limb in the jungle and say that it is not good enough. Get it done!

(**Let's stop here a second!** You should clearly see that your business growth options are endless, so there is no reason you should ever wake up feeling like your are in danger of not bringing home the business-bacon. The only question here should be, "What weapon this week do I want to use to attack my competition with?" So let's continue to build the biggest offline marketing blueprint we can.)

EXISTING CUSTOMERS

FOCUS GROUPS

A huge way to build loyalty and bring in more customers is to have customer focus groups. Invite some of your customers to a call or a meeting. Let them know it is for feedback on what you could be doing to serve them better. Let them know that the food and beer is on you! FYI – that would be a perfect way to get me there! Be prepared to ask them great questions.

Why is this business offline marketing and branding tactic a business home run? Because it accomplishes several invaluable items for your business at once...

Customer Appreciation and Focus Groups:

- Makes the customer feel important. (Building Loyalty)
- Makes them feel heard. (Mega-Retention)
- Helps your marketing because they tell you what they liked. (Customer Persona Gold)
- Helps marketing because they tell you what they don't or didn't like. (Biggest Marketing Gold Nugget) – You have an opportunity to "fix it."
- They spread your brand via word of mouth because you care about them and want to hear their voice! (Business Building Gold)
- Evaporates your competition! (Cementing in the customer's mind that they made the right buying decision.)
- Saves you a ton of money and time! (You can fix holes in your business offerings and zero-in on what worked without guessing) Worth tens of thousands of dollars!

Questions You Should Ask:

- What made you choose us?
- What caught your attention?
- Where did you first hear/find us?
- If we couldn't do business together anymore, what would you miss most?
- What is the one BIG thing we are missing?

- Exactly how would you describe us to a friend?
- What top three things almost stopped you from using us?
- What top three things persuaded you to use us?
- What are your biggest everyday challenges? Anything?
- What could we have done to make your decision easier?

(*Source:* Digital Marketer)

Can you imagine the bags of money this is worth to get these answers? Whatever you just imagined, take ten times that amount and you are still probably short of the value this creates for your business bank account! Not getting customers involved is one of the biggest mistakes a business owner can make. You cannot afford to make this mistake.

> **CEO Non-Negotiable:** Set regular "Customer Appreciation/Focus Groups" to have your brand, marketing and business anointed the King of the Business Jungle!

GIFT CARDS

Immediately *implement a gift card and/or gift certificate program* into your business growth plans. If not, then you are throwing away money! I always say, "Get more while you got 'em!" If you have the sale, why not offer them incentives to grab a gift card/certificate for later or for someone else. This can be free money. You bank cash and sometimes they never even use it. Free Money! Depending on your business type and model, make sure your team and offerings always include gift cards or gift certificates. Make it a part of your process and your company will be worth more money in very short order.

WORD OF MOUTH

And then there was one! You may or may not know it yet, but your best way to become an unstoppable business is by **Word of Mouth** advertising. Your happy customers are your best sales team. If you want to make incrementally more money each business year, then you need to circle the business-wagons around your happy customers. Happy customers can bring you an avalanche on new business, which can turn any business into a profit monster.

Having said that, do you see why I stated earlier that getting a deep understanding of your customer base is so very important? Do this through surveys, customer appreciation initiatives, customer focus groups, customer spotlights, and more. This is very simple business math; the more you focus your efforts on maintaining and creating happy customers, the greater your income becomes as a direct result. This has to be one of your biggest business non-negotiables. Build customer happiness at almost all costs, you will reap income rewards in return.

> "It takes 20 years to build a reputation and five minutes to ruin it. If you think about that, you'll do things differently." -Warren Buffet

Happy customers will scream from the consumer market mountaintops about your products and services. They will put new customers on their backs, in their cars, on boats and trains to make sure the prospects get to your door. How much is that worth? A truckload of money. That is why you need to be hyper-focused on their happiness and you don't know if you don't ask.

Now that you've struck _Customer Gold,_ it is time to _put into motion your Word of Mouth army_.

YOUR SALES TEAM

If you are going to grow your business, then you may have to hire more teammates to help take your business to another level. _Sales are the only way you can stay in business, so hiring great sales people should be a top priority_. Do you ever wonder why sales people make so much money? It is because sales are tough and most individuals are not good at it.

Finding a good sales person is tough to do. You can hire a person for a multitude of reasons, but I suggest that one of the highest weighted qualities to look for in a new sales candidate is _drive_. In fact, Kevin Gaither (V.P. of Inside Sales for ZipRecruiter) says that drive is the most crucial characteristic to look for when hiring a new teammate to help with your sales efforts. You can hire for smarts. You can hire for likability. You can hire for past performance.

Drive is harder to find and bottle up, so look harder for it when searching for your next teammate. Seek to find the right person for your team that has a high drive characteristic, and I'm willing to bet that more often than not, the person you hire with high-drive qualities will meet or exceed your sales expectations.

CEO ACTIVITY: Sale and Marketing Non-Negotiables Creation

- Block out calendar time right now!
- Take this chapter's sales and marketing principles and turn them into your own business marketing and sales non-negotiables.
- Print, laminate and display them for you and everyone to see.
- Set separate time-blocks to shoot videos on your process and non-negotiables to use as training weapons. Use these to ensure sales and marketing consistency!

> **CEO Tip:** Try to hire a person for their drive moreover than other hiring criteria.

Building your best business vision takes time and it is a process, as you can clearly see in this chapter. At a glance, implementing these game changers into your business can seem daunting.

Let's break it down into manageable steps. First, I would begin by sitting down and starting a ten-minute timer on your smartphone. List every marketing topic that you need to investigate or implement. Then I would block out six different two-hour blocks on your calendar to start implementing one item at a time. Do this over a two-week period. So, essentially every week set three different appointments of two hours each to devote to building your business growth masterpiece.

I would put on each appointment, exactly what you want to accomplish in order to be even more focuses during that two-hour block. Again, I would set a timer and get to work at a feverish pitch as if your business life depended on it.

> **CEO Tip:** Document everything. You'll thank me later when it is easy to duplicate the process via leverage because you've given your employees the blueprint.

The key here is to take this chapter's marketing and sales mastery techniques and _build your personal Business Marketing and Sales Non-Negotiables to live by_. My suggestion is that you refer back to this chapter and list out all of the big ticket items in a word document called your "Business Marketing Non-Negotiables" and then spend time ranking them in order of importance. Work from this document to add one to three items in each two-hour time slot you've already blocked out.

While customer satisfaction is at its zenith, I would approach the Word of Mouth maximization the following way:

- Follow up survey, and/or call to get the "why."
- Ask for a testimonial at the right time (product/service timeframe depending).
- Ask for Facebook Likes on your business page.
- Ask for a follow on Twitter.
- Ask for a video testimonial.
- Give them a VIP carrot to make them feel like the cream of the customer crop.
- Let them know you may want to put them on your website (prestige).
- Set up a referral program if appropriate (incentivize).

Take all of this collateral and use it in all of your high traffic hotspots online and offline. You are creating a loyal following and if you are lucky, you will start to create a culture for your brand that is as strong as the Apple brand following.

EXECUTE THE MARKETING!

Take six of these marketing strategies and implement them one at a time. Block out one to two hours on your schedule to get everything in order for each new item, then set a date to execute the strategy. I would like you to do more than one per month, but I will settle for one. The same rules apply as before. Document everything, so you can hand it off to someone else to execute as your business grows.

Sales Increase Tip: Develop reorder forms or a reorder protocol to help with future sales. The key here is to make it easy to do repeat business with you. Whether you hand it to the customer, put it in their shipment and/or add it to your post purchase e-mail; you must develop a repurchase program or you are burning repeat dollars every month.

If you decide to do direct response marketing, then you must re-mail to the leads at least five times to reach the highest response rates. After all, one or two new clients can pay for the total expense to reach the entire audience. Consistency wins and breaks the spirit of the competition, so add the follow up mailings to your calendar the moment the first touch campaign goes out the door. This way you will not even have to think about the next four to five mailings.

> **CEO Tip:** "Go from Offline to Online!"

> **CEO Resource:** How-To Video Resource
> BiggerBusinessBlueprint.com/OffToOn

A big item that can separate your business from the competition is to take the potential customers from your offline marketing to your online tracking lead capture pages. You can do this by adding your e-mail to your offline marketing. What I really want to _BEG_ you to do is buy a domain name (for a little as $9.99) from places like www.godaddy.com and add that "ultra specific" domain name to your marketing materials. (Flyers, Postcards, Letters, Signs, Bandit Signs, Car Magnets and so on.) What I mean by _Ultra Specific Domain Name_ is this: Buy a domain name that completely and utterly makes sense to your perfect customer persona, which spells out _WHY_ they should visit the domain.

Example: Target Customer is "Denver Distressed Home Seller" … then buy a cheap domain name that commands their attention like www.OverpayForDenver.com. Add it to your mailings or road bandit signs that say, "You want to sell your home fast with cash offers? Then visit us here at www.OverpayForDenver.com for 24Hr Cash Offers."

154

You get that? It commands them to go to that site because it speaks directly to their need. When they go to the url it should forward to your lead capture page that talks about cash offers for Denver sellers. It entices them to fill out the form so you get an e-mail with a new lead. (*Any domain company can help you point the domain name you bought to one of your CRM lead capture pages. It takes one minute. There is nothing to contemplate here. This is just pure buy (domain), point (to lead capture page), and shoot everywhere offline!*)

As we get ready to finish our journey through the online and offline jungle, it is my sincere hope that you are super-charged about the future of your business. I hope that I have provided a mountain of invaluable information, with a little step-by-step sprinkled in that fast tracks your retirement plans. All I would ask in return is that when you hit that goal in your business, you blow past your benchmarks, you double the value of your business, and set that retirement party... that I get the first invite to the celebration. I can't wait to shake your hand!

CEO NON-NEGOTIABLE: Don't let the competition win because of your lack of execution!

CEO RESOURCE: Customized Offline Marketing Game Plan

BiggerBusinessBlueprint.com/OfflineMkting

Chapter 8:

Leverage

"The hours that ordinary people waste, extraordinary people leverage." – Robin Sharma

Ah... my favorite entrepreneur business-building weapon. *LEVERAGE!*

One of the greatest keys to experiencing *exponential growth is finding ways to build leverage into the fabric of your business*. This chapter will explore different ways to add elements of leverage to your business to help it run smoother, grow larger, and become more nimble. Leverage is imperative to any modern business that wants to grow in the 21st century. Just like the quote said to start this chapter: ordinary people try to do it all, but extraordinary people strategically use leverage to win.

I always tell business owners the concept of leverage is simple!

"Leverage – You either have it or you don't!"

What I mean is that if you don't have leverage, then the weight and success of the business solely depends on you, which should not be an on-purpose business building strategy! We have all heard the phrase, "They can't seem to get out of their own way!" That is the essence of what *lack of leverage* is for a business owner; not being able to get out of your own way!

An On-Purpose CEO learns quickly that the willful act of taking purposeful measures to apply leverage to their business is one of the fastest ways to the business-growth jackpot. *The faster you can infuse leverage into your business, the faster you can grow while living a more balanced life* versus waking up a slave to your business every single day. Time to get out of your own way and let leverage help you all the way to the bank.

If you want to reach new heights with your business, or you are starting out and you want to poise your business to explode, then you need *LEVERAGE!* When business owners can't get out of their own way and I'm working with them to grow, I usually tell them this:

"Trying to grow a business without the key component of leverage is like farming without seeds. You can stir up a lot of dirt, but in the end you're still left with dirt!" – Jason Palliser

So, let's dig in and explore several ways to introduce more leverage into your business.

LEVERAGE MONEY

The first way to get leverage for your business is to *utilize capital*. Capital can be raised by using your hard-earned cash, by getting a business loan, getting business lines of credit, getting venture capital (but they will typically ask for an ownership stake), or by getting grants. There are more, but we will leave it at that.

If you get capital, what can that do to produce leverage for your business? It can help you place large inventory orders to get cheaper pricing. It can be used to add more workforce. It can be used to upgrade equipment for better output. It can be used to do more marketing (my favorite). It can be used to upgrade software for greater business efficiencies and so on. Also, simply having more capital in the bank can get you cheaper rates on loans, which in turn can save you money. As I am sure you already know, capital makes running the business easier and thus provides you <u>leverage</u>.

LEVERAGE – BUSINESS PARTNERS

Bringing a _business partner_ into your business can give you leverage in a few ways. The first logical way is that the costs can be split between more than one person. This reduces the capital outlay to get things going and reduces your capital at risk.

They can also bring leverage via experience or expertise. You may strategically bring on a partner because they are an expert in the niche your business serves or is looking to serve. This can greatly reduce the time wasted to develop the best efficiency plan and reduce the percentage of costly mistakes. An experienced partner can warn you away from these unseen pitfalls because they have already been down this path before.

A partner can give you a different perspective on future business initiatives, which may help you both collectively come to better business-building decisions. You can potentially partner for a client base (stemming from their sphere of influence). The leverage is that the partner could immediately bring in a crop of customers that would have taken you 12 to 18 months to build.

There is also risk with partnerships as well. You may not see business items eye-to-eye all of the time and that could take away from productivity. If you gain leverage via a partnership, then I strongly suggest that you seek out a business attorney to create an operating agreement. That takes a lot of the guesswork out of the unforeseen challenges which may occur in the future.

(**Disclaimer:** This is purely my opinion. I am not an attorney and this is for educational purposes only. Before you decide to get into a partnership, please seek out an attorney for advice before entering into any agreements for partnering in business.)

> **CEO NON-NEGOTIABLE:** Get an Operating Agreement with "Triggering Events" for later sale or buyouts. Spell out voting and responsibilities. (Otherwise you are assuming.)

Some **Operating Agreement** considerations to discuss with you attorney:

- Triggering events for the sale of the business. (i.e. Death, misappropriations of funds, simply want to part ways, showdown clause.)
- Business Valuation Models – Decide which one you will use if a sale is imminent.
- Each partner's responsibilities.
- Voting rights.
- Spell out who is the Managing Member.
- Set distribution rules.

The point to make here is that you should not go into a

partnership just assuming what each person will do. You should spell it out ahead of time, so that everyone is clear on what the partnership looks like. This allows you to move towards business goals together with confidence.

LEVERAGE - EMPLOYEES

Employees are a great way to produce leverage for your business. The goal is to pay someone a fair wage for what they are going to do for you. This frees you via leverage to perform more *High Dollar Productive Activities* to grow the business even bigger.

You can leverage employees to run day-to-day operations for you. They can sell your products and services for you. They can fulfill your services for you. They can build and deploy your marketing for you. They can tackle prospects and follow up for you to squeeze more new customers out of your lead generation efforts.

Before you add this type of leverage to your business or add new members, please try to adopt some of these hiring considerations to find the best employee fit for your company. The first item to tackle is to perfect your job description in order to attract the right employee. Google has a site called www.rework.withgoogle.com that helps you create the best job practices.

For job description building, they say to separate the description into four areas consisting of job qualifications, the role the applicant would play within your company, their specific responsibilities, and the area they would work within your company. Also try to use action-based verbs to explain their responsibilities such as "plan" and "negotiate" versus "planning and negotiating" which helps fine tune the language of your job offering. Avoid using subjective phrases like "expert at welding" and use more objective phrases like "experience with welding" to help the candidate selection process. When reviewing the applications look for quantifiable indicators such as "increased sales" or "achieved master status" because these are an indication of achievement.

You can hire for a ton of reasons, but the one I personally look to, as a flagship indicator to separate a candidate from the rest of the pack, is the applicant's *drive*. If I can find a person with massive drive, then I will give them the edge every time. I can hire a person with more experience, but in the end, if drive is not one of their highest personal attributes, then their performance may fall short versus a person with higher drive to get to the finish line. Make sure you look to adopt a version of these hiring practices and your business will reap the benefits.

CEO Non-Negotiable: Train Them Well and Incentivize Them!

If you have employees or are going to hire employees in the future, I would beg you to slow down and train them well. The better you train them, the better the return on your employee investment. They can be your best assets if you put the right time and energy into them. I would also set clear goals for employees and set benchmarks to hit. People tend to work harder when they are working towards something versus just performing a task in exchange for a wage. And lastly, I would incentivize them for their hard work. Incentives can be bonuses, extra time off, advancement, raises, simple designation/status increase, and (if applicable) profit sharing. These are items I would plan to put in motion to get the most leverage out of your employees.

LEVERAGE – INTERNSHIPS

Colleges are filled with thousands of potential leverage partners. In today's college world, most students have to complete some form of internship before they are allowed to graduate. Remember, we are talking about building a bigger business on-purpose! That is why are you here! If you want to make more money and grow a bigger business on-purpose, then let me ask you a vey simple business question.

CEO Question: *"If most college students need to do an internship before they graduate, then why are they not working for you?"*

The answer is that they should be working for you. I would make it your CEO mission to have at least one intern working for your business within the next 30 to 60 days. Before I let you go crazy with one of my favorite leverage strategies, I should probably give you some best practices and approaches to hiring interns.

Before I hit you with some intern hiring best practices and strategies, let's list a few things that an intern could do for you depending on what type of business you run. An intern could:

- Research competitors.
- Be a secret shopper and report back how your company handled them as a new customer.
- Create follow up e-mails for you.
- Place flyers out strategically at venues where your perfect customer prospects congregate.
- Compile data for you.
- Create marketing research folders for you.
- Visit social sites for you and set up your profiles.
- Research getting our products cheaper for you, so there are higher profit margins.
- Find charity events, local fairs, church fairs, trade shows, conventions and send the list to you, so you can

look to attack these for exposure and customers.
- Obviously they can attack college campuses and venues for you.
- Run online ads for you: CraigsList, Google, Facebook, and more.
- Get written and video testimonials for you to add to your website, social media, and more.
- Place bandit signs for you.

Hopefully you get the picture.

So let's talk about some _best practices and approaches to hiring interns_. The first place I would start is to visit a university website and use their search bar to type in "Internship" and see what pops up. It may tell you the procedures to post for internship positions with your company. Or the website may have a spot where students have posted they are seeking internships. It just depends on the way the university has it set up. You can also look up different university departments and find a phone number. Simply call to ask how you can get in front of their students with your internship opportunities. You can even visit the campus or campuses and place flyers at their student common areas or dorms.

Your next step would be to construct your internship ad to attract suitors. (A word to the wise here, depending on what you want them to do for your company, you may not want to post just anything to hire them. What I mean is, they may want to intern with you, but if your description is not a "good match" for their degree program, their advisor's office may not give the student credit towards finishing their degree.

In light of this new discovery, I would write your internship offering to match students' different areas of study. Such as, you may want them visit websites for you and collect competitor information, but you may want to list the internship as data research, or market demographics, or economic market research. If they are going to help you run the office, then you can list the internship as accounting and business management, and not list it as cashier and trash duties. I think you get my drift.

Typically the student has to fulfill some sort of timeframe to complete their internship. Sometimes it is a certain number of hours worked or a time period of weeks or months. Whatever the requirement is, you typically will have to sign-off on some paperwork to confirm they completed their internship with your company.

When you hire them, pay them. You don't have to pay them much, but in today's world you should pay them something. It is not like the old days where it was just free labor. Another standard practice I would add to the internship program is to incentivize them for good work. If you put it together well, you may even keep them working to grow your profitability after they have completed their internship.

When you train them, train them well. You'll reap the rewards. Remember, they are supposed to get something out of the internship as well, so teach them about your business and how it works. Make them understand and give them what they are supposed to get when they do their internship, which is more knowledge.

One of the biggest reasons why I want you to train them well is this: As they are drawing near the end of their internship, I want you to pull them aside and tell them, "The last task I want you to perform before I sign off on your internship, is to _TRAIN YOUR REPLACEMENT_!"

Stop! Wait a second here! You read this correctly. Imagine they have 20 hours left before their internship is done or one week left. Then imagine telling them that you will sign off on their internship as soon as they find and train their replacement;

whether or not that takes them two hours or one day. If you train them well and then set their last task as training their replacement, then <u>that means you could have an endless supply of interns that run on autopilot forever</u>. How is that for *LEVERAGE*?

I would set a goal to have at least two or three interns working for you at all times. After all, they have to complete one to graduate. Why not have them working for you? They should be.

LEVERAGE - VIRTUAL ASSISTANTS

The Ultimate Leverage Weapon! Virtual Assistants!

My absolute favorite income producing leverage is utilizing Virtual Assistants! Using V.A.s can be a game-changing competitive advantage over your competition. The first advantage is that most business owners don't truly understand the concept, so they never even explore the possibility of using virtual assistants. Second, they cannot get past the concept of working with someone they cannot see to help them close more business.

The fact is that in today's world, the Internet connects thousands of business owners every month to very qualified V.A.s, who are willing to work cheap. Your business can benefit from these people. It is my job to help you explore this mega-leverage strategy and pull you into the 21st century, along with bags of extra income.

<u>This is my FAVORITE part of the book! Hands Down!</u>

V.A. Leverage!

I'm gonna do something I've never done before, so pay attention!

(Before I change your life here, let's get past your mental block! I hear this all of the time from entrepreneurs who cannot get out of their own way!)

"But Jason! Will they really work super cheap and where do they live since I can't see them?"

We will tackle the "working cheaper" in a second, but I want to smash the last part of the question about "I can't see them." Read up! Get out of your own mental way! Who cares if you cannot sit down to have coffee with your virtual assistant? Let me paint the picture why you should not care if you can see them or not and I will use my business as an example.

I have tons of clients that I have met "one time" for less than an hour to review investment real estate planning, yet after that one-time meeting, I have done 5, 10, 15, 20 or more deals with them without ever seeing them again! Do you get that hiring a V.A. you do not see daily or weekly is the exact same thing? In fact, I have clients that I have done tons of deals for who I have never met and would not know if they were standing right next to me in a coffee shop! Just because I have not met them, does that mean that I cannot crush the items they hire me to do for them like a monster? Of course not!

167

Hiring a V.A. that can produce results and give you leverage cheap is no different than me getting an email from a client and getting the job done!

You don't have to have coffee with your virtual assistant. They may not even like coffee!

Now let's first tackle why virtual assistants are willing to work so cheap for you. I hear all of the time from my clients and trainees the following statement, "I just can't believe they will work so cheap!" One reason they work cheap is because they are specialists at what they do. If they can do it without leaving their home and use their skill set in mass production, then they can afford to do it cheaper.

As an example, some VAs are already very good a creating Facebook Business Pages for clients. They can probably get one done in three minutes and then spend another 25 minutes polishing it up into a super-sexy business page that commands attention. On the flip side of this, imagine what type of time and effort it may take you to do the same thing. My guess would be hours and even more hours of mental anguish to just get the process started. Chances are that the V.A. has already produced 20 new FB Pages for clients and s/he only charges $5 per business page.

The next big reason they may work cheaper for you is that they may live in an area or country which the wages for comfortable living are much lower than our standards here in North America. As an example, a customer service representative that lives and works in the Philippines makes an average of $213,236 PHP (Philippine Peso) per year according to www. payscale.com. The conversion rate to US Currency as of October 31st, 2015 is equal to roughly $4,574 per year. Do you see why you might gain massive leverage by hiring a virtual assistant that is willing to make sales calls and follow up calls for you for two to six dollars per hour? And, they might be the best call sales rep you'll ever have. Got your attention, don't I?

Another very enticing _benefit of leveraging a virtual assistant is that it is "a task based relationship,"_ which is different from hiring normal employees. With a V.A. you no longer have to feel the pressure of keeping a person employed, unlike when you have a normal employee. When the V.A. completes a task, you pay them and the relationship is done until you need them again. Furthermore, if you hire them from sites like Fiverr.com or Upwork.com, you get to review how they performed once the task is completed.

Imagine getting graded on every task your perform for someone. I'll bet that you would work harder. The beauty with the online V.A. sites is that you get to see the reviews before you hire them. It is like having a ranking system to help you choose the right person to help you. Versus regular employees, imagine how many thousands of dollars you can save in salary, benefits, and more with a V.A. helping you run your business. Using this leverage can give you an instant profitability boost!

Now that I have your complete attention, let's talk about what they can do for you. Remember, you are hiring specialists for almost any task you need performed. That means when you post to hire a V.A. on one of these websites, you are going to get responses from V.A.s and not responses from accounting specialists. So again, what can they do for you when you need them to?

Virtual Assistants can...
- be your bookkeeper.
- be your marketing director.
- research competitors and create folders with competitor materials.

- join online groups to interact with your perfect customer personas. From there they direct traffic to your website, lead capture pages, or to call you.
- build marketing pieces and create graphics.
- write articles for you.
- build your follow up sequences.
- run your CRM for you, set up auto-responder e-mail and contact management.
- be your customer service reps.
- be your post-sale satisfaction survey team.
- be your executive assistant. (i.e. handle calendars, booking flights, booking hotels.)
- be your secret shopper to make sure your company is delivering.
- research new suppliers to get cheaper product pricing.
- track your marketing and split-testing.
- manage event coordination.
- manage online meetings and send invites.
- confirm appointments and subscriptions.
- create videos for you and edit videos.
- manage products and product offerings to adjust pricing when needed.
- handle file and transaction management.
- buy and ship holiday gifts.
- transcribe voicemails, recorded meetings, podcasts and videos.
- support and manage support tickets.
- handle recruitment.
- organize resumes, verify employment, and references.
- handle payroll.

You get the point right? To get the ball rolling, I suggest you pick two to four items on this list and post the tasks on one of the V.A. websites. Please note that I conveyed, "Post the task" and did not say that you had to hire anyone. All you are simply doing is starting the conversation. You are still in control of whether or not you end up hiring a V.A. or not. The point I'm trying to drive home with you here is that you need to see how the process works and just how easy it is. I know that once you do and you actually strike a deal to hire a V.A. for a task, then you will be in love with V.A. services and you will never look back.

The final V.A. nugget of knowledge I will impart to you centers on how to interact with them to help you find the best match. When you post for a job or task offering, I would always ask them for sample work if warranted, to see if you think their work is a match for what you want. Also, I think it goes without saying, but read their reviews to make sure their past service to other business owners has been favorable.

Lastly, I would always put a buzz phrase towards the end of your ad that asks them to respond back to you with that exact buzz phrase to make sure they read your entire ad. Pretty sneaky, huh? You want to make sure they did not just read the first couple of lines and clicked to respond without knowing exactly what you want them to do.

V.A. Test: Hire a V.A.! Your 21st century business will thank you for it. For fun, hire a V.A. to call you next Tuesday at 4pm sharp and tell you how awesome you are for $1. Just to prove to you how it works and how they can help you make more money while spending less to do it.

CEO MEGA RESOURCE:

<u>My "Bigger Business Blueprint" Thank You</u>:

<u>Never Before Access To My Private Virtual Assistant Team.</u>

<u>www.leveragemate.com</u>

Schedule Your Free 1-on-1 Interview with my VAs to grow your business.

Experience Leverage That Helps Me Run 18 + Income Streams.

LEVERAGE – TECHNOLOGY AND AUTOMATION

Leverage through technology and automation is a must for an On-Purpose CEO and a must if you want to truly become a 21st century business. Oh, and for the record, we _are_ in the 21st century, so this is kind of a non-negotiable. There is no greater leverage for a business than technology.

Shouldn't you be able to grab more customers and marketshare while you sleep? Of course you can and should! How does that happen? Technology and Automation! In this section we will explore what automation is possible for your business and what should be some of your biggest business to-do items when you finish building your bigger business blueprint.

There are so many game changing business opportunities here that I'm just going to start with the no-brainers. _A website_ *is a must.* If you don't have one, then set one up. Review the instructions in chapter eight if you need a refresher. I recommend choosing a WordPress template for ease-of-use.

Once you've bought a website template, find a V.A. that specializes in WordPress to build it for you. They can add your logos and initial pages to get the ball rolling. They can do this for anywhere from $50 to $500 to get it done. Once it is done, they will forward your website to the $10 website domain name you bought and you will be up and running.

Your website is a must because now the world can find you 24-hours a day and at their leisure. Today's consumers want you when they want you, and not when you decide you are open for business. This is what your website solves.

My favorite technology for modern business owners to leverage is utilizing a Customer Relationship Management (CRM) tool. It can run your marketing, your customer acquisition tracking, and your sales management initiatives like a machine. Not all CRMs are created equal, so make sure you choose one that gives you the ability to:

- Create lead capture pages.
- Set easy follow up e-mail campaigns.
- Automatically categorizes your leads.
- Creates new contacts for you automatically.
- Develop and allow you to attach lead pages to your website (pretty much all websites today allow you to add your CRM lead pages to the website).
- Contact management – batch e-mails, batch letter printing, customer reminders, employee reminders, and trigger automatic customer service team reminders.

This allows you to focus on growing the business because your CRM is following up, tracking productivity, capturing leads, putting leads in the right follow up sequences, and more.

Some game changing automation items your CRM can automatically do for you:

- It can confirm purchases for you and the customer.
- It can follow up with a new lead in less than one second and ask them "Qualifying Questions" to categorize how HOT or NOT the lead is and you can sell accordingly.
- Notify you and team members the exact moment when a potential new customer has become your lead.
- Notify you when the potential customer has finished your nurture campaign and has NOT done what you want, so you can be proactive immediately and try to convert them.
- It can tell you which marketing pieces are winning, so you can tweak the others to get better results. (Priceless!)
- It can e-mail all of your customers at once to tell them about your new products and services to get an immediate spike in sales.

(Also, know that any good CRM has support. Typically they have videos on every little function they offer, so you can watch, pause, do it and complete your set up very easily. They want to help you. You are paying them money to use their automation services and they want to keep you as a happy customer. In short, you are not on your own!)

Leverage your social presence easily by using tools like www. hootsuite.com and www.ifttt.com. Use them to automatically place your products, services and offers to several places at once. They can also let you schedule your posts. Example: you have several offers that you want to get out to places like Facebook, LinkedIn, Twitter, and other sites. These tools let you sit down once and schedule which ones go out now and which ones go out later.

With these tools your offers can be everywhere for weeks at a time, dripping out to the public when you strategically want and it was all scheduled in one sitting. The mega-leverage is that you can be efficient and take 30 minutes to explode your online offerings for weeks on end, allowing you to move onto the next business-building item on your growth to-do list.

My biggest business owner plea yet is coming right now. _Please put automating your business at the top of your to-do list. This will be a game changer that runs income through your bank accounts effortlessly for as long as you want it to_.

This is the 21st century. Do not give your competition the edge by doing everything the old-fashioned way. Once this is set up, it will run independent of you.

THE MENTAL SHIFT TO INNOVATION

Imagine _your CRM is an employee that never sleeps, never asks for a day off, never forgets to collect leads, always stays organized, and never misses an opportunity to follow up_. What would you pay that employee? My bet is thousands and thousands of dollars. Guess what? It may only cost you about $30 to $50 a month and you don't have to offer them benefits. Heck, you might get two or three CRMs for that type of loyalty and leverage. Get it done ASAP!

> **CEO ACTIVITY: Automate What?**
> - Spend five minutes listing out all of the business items you might want to automate.
> - Then place them in order of importance to you.
> - Lastly, think about what needs to be in place first to make a priority action item list.

Let this CEO activity serve as your automation roadmap specific to your business and business initiatives. It can easily convey to others what you need help with, so they can make it happen.

Don't worry! I promise I have a process that you will see later to help you become an action-item champion, so create some to-do items and hold on tight. You'll see why my consulting clients think I don't sleep and why they are jacked-up when I get my hands on their business! It is coming! I promise!

LEVERAGE DUPLICATE YOURSELF

As an On-Purpose CEO, you need to think about _duplicating yourself_. As previously stated, you cannot be the bottleneck that slows your company's growth. Honesty is the best policy here, so let's admit that you cannot be available all of the time.

When business decisions are being slowed down by waiting for answers from the top, income suffers and customers are lost. Leveraging your skill set to others and training your replacement is a way to keep the business in a position to grow independent of you. Preparing to remove yourself from the business-growth equation allows it to make progress on its own. It helps the business health not to be interdependent on you for survival. You need to train your equal and slowly prepare your duplicate to help with business decisions. This frees you to live the entrepreneur life that you want to live.

Duplicating yourself can create massive business leverage for you because it frees you to work on more "rainmaking" activities that can really ramp up your brand and business income. The duplicate can now focus on the day-to-day activities when called upon and you (hopefully the company's best asset) can focus on growth.

Make sure you also _incentivize them_ and give them opportunities to help motivate them to push your business net worth even higher. Incentivizing is a polite way to make sure that the person doesn't feel like you are just handing them your business headaches. It shows that you're placing more value on their contribution, which typically motivates them to want to take the company growth even higher.

A few things to consider when training your clone. _Train them well_. The more you can train them and dig deep on the front-end, the better the results on the business back-end. Don't skimp and don't leave out details. Get granular with your efforts into training them because when you do, the result is a strong sense of confidence that will pay off in the end. You can start incrementally, letting your protégé make good business decisions for you. You are free to work on _High Dollar Productive Activities_ and let the business run with less of you in the mix. _Leverage victory!_

Document everything well, so you can rinse and repeat the process later when you leverage even more talent. Video everything you can about your process and philosophy for the business. This ensures consistency in the delivery of company policy and best practices for others coming into your business fold.

Please Note: You may be somewhat of an _admitted conspiracy theorist_ who is thinking, "If I train them well, then they may take business from me later!" I'll concede that the concern is legitimate. As a smart business owner, I would simply consult with an attorney about the putting together documents to protect your business when you bring on a protégé.

Consult with your attorney first of course, but you can use business protection practices like non-compete documents, non-circumvent documents, non-solicitation documents, non-emulate documents, and more if needed. This can help to reduce the risk associated with handing over the keys to the business-castle.

Below are some documents you want to discuss with an attorney to see if they should be signed:

- Non-Compete Agreement
- Non-Solicitation Agreement
- Non-Emulate Agreement

LEVERAGE – BUSINESS CONSULTANTS AND MENTORS

The last type of leverage that you may want to tap into is _business consulting or mentoring_. This can be invaluable to increasing the net worth of your business. Someone who has "been there, done that" can streamline your business and bring the right growth initiatives into focus in a more concise order.

It is usually ego that gets in the way of business growth through smart collaboration. I've seen it first hand, where a client is holding their business back due to their ego and not getting out of their own way.

No one knows everything in business, therefore seeking outside help is the mark of a truly smart business mind!

In fact this ego analogy fits one of my former business partners like a glove. They could not get out of their own way to save their business life and therefore were hurting their true potential to grow. Don't make the same mistake in your business. Get out of your own way and grab a mentor to collaborate. If you don't, it could cost you millions! Capturing this type of leverage can be a life-changing event, but typically _only the strong can put their ego aside to bottle this type of leverage magic_.

This type of leverage can be more difficult to find. While finding a successful business owner you can learn from shouldn't be very difficult; finding a successful business mentor that has the time to coach you (while running their successful businesses), may be a different story.

Consultants are different. They get paid to help you grow strategically. This is a good reason why _finding a good business consultant_ may be your best bet. They get paid to get you out of your own way. They get paid to give you a better perspective and more business growth opportunity options.

Finding a business consultant or mentor can accelerate your business tremendously. Why? A good business consultant or mentor can help you create a clear vision of where you want to take your business. They have been there and already worked through some of the growing pains that new and existing businesses inevitably face. As you look to take the next big step for business growth, they can build better paths for you to get there with less effort and less cost.

A mentor or consultant can simply give you a fresh point of view and be objective to help you come to smarter solutions in your business. They can save you thousands in business inefficiencies and business-oopsies.

The value is almost unfathomable. Imagine a business consultant or mentor that can look at your company and shave 30% off your trial and error business journey to retirement. Now imagine they can carry you right out of harms way and fast track your path to more income in much less time. Try to place a leverage value on that! Whatever number you come up with in your head, I would triple it and you would still probably fall short of their real business world value.

Consulting/Mentoring Leverage Example: As an example, I was graced with an appointment with a very smart businessman that evaluates companies, invests in them, and builds them up for sale later. He actually looked at a company that I was building with a partner. He liked what he saw and he gave some words of advice. He gave us tips on how to be more valuable.

I later saw him in an airport and updated him on where the company has gone since our previous meetings and conveyed some challenges we were experiencing in the business. Again, he provided solid advice. I took the advice and decided to execute the sale of that company. He not only helped me make the right decision, but also helped me get free to grow other business ventures even more. He could objectively see what I could not. I was too close to the day-to-day grind in my business to see what he clearly saw.

The moral of the business story here is to leverage other successful business owners' collective wisdom to help you make smarter business decisions. In fact, I would make it a point to run big business decisions by other business owners for a different and unbiased opinion to help you make better decisions.

If I could go back in time to give myself advice, I would gladly write a big check for that wisdom and also slap me silly (if needed) to get me out of my own way with some "wisdom leverage." It would pay my businesses dividends multiple times over and give me leverage that is almost impossible to put a price tag on.

LEVERAGE – THE CONCLUSION

Leverage is critical if you really want to maximize your true growth potential. The business owners that consistently seek new ways to bring more leverage to their businesses will be the ones poised for the greatest growth. The faster you grab it, the faster you reach your business income targets. Today's technology leverage has made it easier than ever to reduce man-hours into minutes. With more capital in your pocket, you have leverage to explore even greater expansion options.

Leveraging _virtual assistants_ is my favorite way to immediately give you increased "on-time" opportunity to close more business while all of the other items important to business success are being handled. If you have not set up your one-on-one VA interview yet, then do it now at www.leveragemate.com. Unload business tasks onto your new tireless business team, which is ready to work for anywhere from $4 to $8 per hour. Better hurry! Your competition isn't doing everything, so why are you?

Finally, _business consultant or mentor leverage_ can help eliminate guesswork and deliver wisdom that otherwise could be a costly item to attain and usually comes at the expense of your pocketbook. To assess whether a business consultant or mentor would be beneficial, simply look around the boardroom. If you look at your business and the team built around it and you are the smartest one in the room, then you are in the wrong room, my friend. Leverage the expertise of the battle-tested business owners that have been in the game awhile. They can help give you the blueprint to a successful winning business team that can shape your bright business future in an impactful, positive way.

Make infusing leverage into your business the standard and not the exception. Leverage can set your growth on a meteoric rise that a "one man/woman band" can only dream about. Doing "it" all yourself is a thing of the past. Speed kills and leverage delivers it!

Chapter 9:

Bigger Business Growth Strategies

THE FINISHING TOUCHES

As we get near the _Bigger Business On Purpose_ finish line, it is time to put on the finishing touches. We've covered virtually every aspect of your business. This chapter is devoted to keeping your business running at the highest purposeful clip that it can. We will cover some income maximization strategies and best practices that will put your business in the winner's circle.

The way to uncover some hidden income is to ask yourself two fundamental questions: "_What can I do to maximize my opportunity with every person my business touches?_" and, "_What can I do to run my business more efficiently to maximize profitability?_" This is the final step to unlocking income opportunity that most competitors never reach. Sometimes it is just the little tweaks that make the difference.

So, just like a racing team that tests and tweaks their engine to squeeze out as much performance as they can, we will explore some business tweaks that can take your modern business to the next level with skillfully engineered precision. After all, *"There would be no such phrase as the winning formula if everyone got it right the first time around."* It is time to test, tweak, and explore to find your best winning business formula.

CEO TIP: Prioritize! "Work on Your "E's" in the right order! Earnings over Ease! Big payoff items first, not just the easy business to-do items!"

- Jason Palliser

SALE/INCOME MAXIMIZATION EXPLORATION

Having laid the foundation for a bigger and better on-purpose business, now we are seeking to find the right twists and turns to your business operation to reach optimum income potential. Let's start by exploring some sales and income tweaking to find the best winning formula.

When you have everything in place to bring business income in the door, winning businesses look even deeper for income and sales opportunities. It goes along the same lines we learned earlier about split-testing your marketing to never stop improving. The same goes with maximizing your income potential as well. *It doesn't take much for a business to go "from mediocre to meteoric" by testing small incremental tweaks to unlock hidden income.* Never stop testing to improve and your opportunity will never stop growing as well.

AUTOMATION

The first items I would like you to look at for improvement

are the sales process and lead funnel. You want to examine the customer experience to _make the process easier_. Test your business mind by listing out the typical steps a customer takes to buy from you. Look to simplify by reducing the steps to purchase. One way to reduce steps is to _take any offline processes and try to implement online solutions._

Example: You return calls to prospects and convince them to buy. A sales increasing solution could be to change your standard voicemail to include verbiage that they can finish the purchase by visiting your website at (whatever your site name is) and click on "XYZ" for immediate processing.

Note: _They can still buy from you the regular way, but now you've given another option that could increase your sales dramatically. Don't make it tough to buy from you. Deep inside you probably know this but it bears repeating: By the time you get back with the prospect, the competition may have already satisfied their need. By tweaking the process you can close more business instead of procedurally losing it._

> **CEO NON-NEGOTIABLE:** Make it easy to do business with you!

TEST OFFERINGS

Another income boosting refinement to your offerings may be to simply _give more to get more_. Provide more value than anticipated to spike your sales performance. Go the extra mile and look to add some nominally valued offers to spike sales. In essence, you give a little to get more sales.

With the tracking tools I've mentioned, it can be easy to _track which offers produce more sales_ and continue to tweak until you find the perfect offering formula. Remember, offering more does not always have to cost extra. Depending on your product and service offerings, you can also add a one-on-one session with you or your team. To become your customer, the prospect has to decide to buy, which means they are weighing their options. Tip the scales in your favor by adding more value to your offers.

An added value example could be that your company sells software. To increase your sales conversions you may want to offer a private one-on-one session with you or your team. Let them know you're going to help them kick start performance with personal attention. Or maybe you sell furniture and sell protection guard services separately. Try combining them as a value added extra, when the cost may be minimal to you and your result may be a 15% increase in sales. Pro Tip: Add these tweaks to your order form so customers can just check a box! Sometimes your sales team may forget to ask, so including it on the order form is a reminder!

I would test as many different offerings you can to try to find the best winning sales formula. Your attention to detail and purposeful testing is what can send your sales into overdrive. _Remember, even if some tweaks are not winners, the knowledge you gain is invaluable, because one-by-one you are eliminating guesswork. It is simple. Stick with what works and tweak what doesn't_. Your bank account will respond positively to your willingness to search for the perfect offerings.

REPEAT SALES

The logical wrinkle I would add to increase your business income is to _"strike while the iron is hot,"_ or in other words, offer something else to purchase within the first 30 days of gaining a new customer. There are a couple of reasons for this. One reason is that the new customer is typically at their happiness-zenith right after they buy, so now is a good time to add some additional sales. The second reason is _statistics show that your customer is typically seven to ten times more likely to buy again from you within the first 30 days after the initial sale versus the rest of the calendar year_, so turn your business offerings and income potential initiatives into purely a numbers game. Utilizing these statistics in your sales offering system can produce more income. All you have to do is construct your sales opportunity funnels and customer follow up accordingly. Follow up early and often to maximize customer ROI.

Happy customers and customer loyalty are business income gold. To do your part as the CEO of your business, you need to construct the best post-purchase thank you and customer touch process on planet Earth. Why, you might ask? Here is why. The _White House Office of Consumer Affairs published that happy and loyal customers are worth a whopping ten times more than your average customer_. If they are happy, you can potentially increase your revenue tenfold. Furthermore, statistics say that the percentage of selling a new prospect is between 5%–20%, versus selling an existing customer, which is between 60%–70%. Is that worth rolling out the red carpet to your new customers? Uh...YES!

Prepare the best customer touch plan on Earth. Keep the competition at the starting line and eliminate their chance to grab your customer's attention. A good thank you campaign can mitigate buyers remorse, resolve product or offer confusion, cement your brand in their mind, bring you referrals, and help you spend less to make more money. After all, selling to an existing client is way less costly than the time, effort, and money it takes to acquire new customers. Any way you try to slice it, customer thank you and follow up makes you more money and builds your brand. Make them feel special and reap the business rewards.

My suggestion would be to _make the thank you campaign and_

post sale follow up multifaceted. Touch base via e-mail, phone call, video thank you, social media thank you, and more. The better you are at reaching them everywhere, the stronger the bond between your brand and the customer. Do little things like adding buy-links into your e-mail signature for other products or complimentary services that help maximize your customer value.

REFERRALS AND REWARDS

Now that you have built some kick-ass customer loyalty protocols into your non-negotiable business growth process, it is time to give the loyal customers an incentive to bring you new customers. This can be in the form of discounts on their future purchases for referring a customer. It can be a rewards point-system for each new client referred to you. They could also get a "member of the month" spotlight on your website after so many referrals. Just the prestige alone is enough for some customers to start referring.

I used the spotlight strategy with customers of my real estate software and they went crazy over the recognition. My partner and I basically rewarded them for getting social and sharing with others. They got their name and business anchored on our website and got massive peer exposure. The spotlight program did not cost me anything and brought great referrals! Brainstorm some incentives you can offer for loyalty and referrals, and roll out the plan as soon as you can. Your customer value will skyrocket and your customer retention will strengthen.

DOWN-SELL

Let's face it, losing customer sales is what you do! At first glance you probably didn't like the statement, but facts are facts. Didn't we already say that you have a 5% – 20% chance of selling the prospect? Yes, we did! So, another income strategy to deploy is down-selling the prospect just to get the business. Before they leave, make a last ditch effort to capture something, such as a smaller sale, just to get them in the door. It only makes sense, correct? We just stated that when they buy they are 60% -70% more likely to buy additional products and services from you. So, get them in the door.

Find strategic ways to cut the price of your offering and add a scaled-down version that makes it easier to buy and capture more paying customers. Don't let them leave at all costs. You worked too hard to their attention and to get them close to the finish line. Help push them through with different offers, then you can hit them up after the fact with some up-sell offers in your thank you campaigns. _Give a little to get more._

INCREASE ONLINE BUSINESS REPUTATION

- 90% Trust Peer Reviews
- 97% Trust Online Reviews to be Accurate
- 92% Trust Online Reviews vs. Sales Clerks
- Anchor more sales with online social proof!
- Be in control of your brand!
- Competition is waiting to pounce!

Strengthen your online business reputation. Your sales depend on it. This one is harder to quantitatively track, but we need to make sure that your brand and online presence is rock-solid to anchor in more sales. Most new customers look online before they make their buying decision, so make sure you put your best business-foot forward online, so you don't suffer the decreased sales consequences.

It is a fact that you can't make everyone happy no matter how hard you try, but you can work hard to turn that "frown upside down!" Newell Lenger from the "Understanding Customers" camp, states that it takes roughly 12 positive experiences to turn an unhappy customer experience back into a positive light. In addition, the White House Office of Consumer Affairs estimates that bad customer news travels twice as fast as good news. Your company must spread the positive word across your online presence in order to anchor the overwhelming positive experience potential clients need to see.

It is estimated that three in five customers are ready to try a new brand in pursuit of a better experience. Hence, the reason you must have the best customer thank you process on Earth, coupled with an online arsenal of good product reviews and testimonials. You can put your business attention anywhere you want, but putting your attention to the right items like customer thank you funnels can help you retire on top.

Your sales depend on what people see and feel online. The numbers back it up. _It is estimated that 90% of consumers trust peer reviews over your marketing_. Whether it is true or not, consumers also trust online reviews to be accurate, so you better spread the happy customer mojo socially and strategically on your website. The more good news you have out there in the online jungle, the better your sales will be. And just in case you weren't convinced yet, _a whopping 92% of potential customers trust online reviews over your sales clerk_. You better pay attention to what people are saying about you online because your business life depends on it. If you see a negative remark, I would look to kill that person with kindness and turn them into a brand advocate. No matter how long it takes, it will be worth its weight in gold to turn that negative customer into a happy customer.

Your brand reputation is your business shield. Keep it strong online with positive reviews, testimonials, great content, user-friendly online tools/websites, and more. Your competition is waiting for you to fall and they will step right over you to grab your prospects' hand if you let your shield slip. Pay attention to your brand online. You can't make everyone happy, but you can die trying.

PROFIT MAXIMIZATION EXPLORATION

Sometimes building a bigger business is done without increasing your sales numbers. You can explore other items directly related to your profitability in order to build a better annual bottom line. Let's check out a few profitability-increasing strategies to explore within your business.

COST-CUTTING

The first one is to set a one-on-one appointment with your CPA and explore every option to reduce your tax liability. (**Disclaimer:** _I am not a CPA, nor do I play one on TV. This is for educational purposes only. Before making any changes to your business model, consult with your CPA professional to make choices appropriate for your situation._) Ask about being able to deduct expenses. For example, you may be able to deduct 100% of meals and entertainment instead of 50% if your expenditures are in efforts to gain new business from prospective customers. Check into it. Ask about relocating your business to a state where there is not a state tax. An example of this would be Florida. This is one way to make some procedural changes that may help you become more profitable.

Another profit center to explore is bulk pricing (depending on your business). You may only utilize 40% of what is needed to get a bulk discount on a monthly basis, but explore the savings if you collect three months of inventory upfront. Calculate how much more profit per customer is realized by buying more upfront. If you know you're going to sell it, then why not buy more of it for pricing breaks? You should do it. Again, depending on what you sell, this can increase your profits by 10% – 25% if done correctly.

Want to get seriously creative? Talk to your competitors and see if they want to bulk purchase together with you for even deeper discounts. Just because they are in the same niche that you are in, does not mean you can't work together and be more profitable. You can even talk to them about overflow services. If you can't meet demand, you contract out to your competitor to provide fulfillment for an agreed upon fee. This is a win-win for both businesses. If you do this, then I would make sure you execute a non-solicitation agreement so there is no confusion on whose customer the client is in the future.

TEST PRICING

Increase profits be increasing your price. Most business owners are scared to try this, but you don't know until you try. Furthermore, if you don't try, then you are letting fear be the tail that wags the dog.

Price testing is the only real way to find out if you are selling yourself and business short. A strategic way to do this is to add some more value to the offering that gives the price increase some justification. You may find that your sales stay the same, which at first glance by the Untrained-CEO-Eye, seems to be a failure. But, what if you raised the price by 18% and the sales didn't take a dip. You've just increased your business profitability by 18% a year by split-testing offers. That is a business home run in my book.

Finally, in an effort to squeeze more profitability out of your business, you can implement some product and service bundling. If your business model is more conducive to it, try an immediate post-sale offering to increase the value of each new customer coming into your business.

For example, if you sell customized apparel, then every time you get a customer shirt order try to add a hat. The hat may have a smaller profit margin, but it is a tag-on to gain more income. Or as soon as they go to finalize the order, hit them with a deeply discounted offer to double their order or hit them with the hat offer then. The key here is to make it your business to be in the "Sales offer testing business!" *He or she, whom never stops testing, never stops improving!*

EXECUTION MAXIMIZATION

- Set shorter goals. (90 days or less)
- Calendar Blocking. (with initiatives added)
- Accountability Partnering.
- Get rid of time wasters.

The devil is in the details, correct? If you were smart enough to read through this book, then I'm sure I have planted the seeds for positive change in your business. I congratulate you for taking action to explore new ways to build a bigger business on-purpose! I am also certain that anyone who pick up this business changing book can get lost in the "I don't know what to do first" jungle!

Time to explore some items to help you become the most dangerous business owner on the planet. *It starts and stops with execution!* If you want to win the business battle over your competition, then you need to become an execution machine. The fastest way to win is to execute!

> **CEO Non-Negotiable:** Nothing should ever get in the way of my business execution!

"That right! I said it! If you want to kill the competition, become an executioner!"

Nothing separates your business from the competition faster than execution. The problem for most business owners is that they do not know where to start. They simply do not have any real standard practices in place to help them stay focused and execute. It is no wonder that most businesses do not have their presence in more than three or four places online.

As a modern business they are simply throwing money in the trash, not because they don't know they need to grow their brand, but rather because they don't plan to execute. Most business owners want to leap from good to great (or even world class!) but are held back by lack of execution.

Let's simplify things a little here. If you blocked out time to _execute just one business initiative per week_, then at the end of one year you would have knocked out 52 business growth initiatives. Do you think your business would be bigger? Of course it would, but most business owners carry around a to-do list for months without executing it! Why? Because they fill their time with busy work. Don't fall into the "I'm busy, but not purposefully busy" trap. Remember, this book is about building a bigger business blueprint and we have the plans; now it is time to explore the process to execute it. Time to infuse your process with some execution elements that can help fast track your business.

The first step to easier execution is to list our your growth initiatives and purposefully calendar block to execute the items. I would prioritize and plan to execute one to two items per week and _block sacred business-building time on your calendar_ and _do it without any interruptions_.

As another tip, I would block out separate times to execute the one to two items per week. Do not block out half of a day or an entire day to cross the items off of your to-do list. It will never happen. As a modern business owner, there are too many distractions (no matter how well intended we are) for you to disconnect for an entire day. Do it in chunks. I would tell you to block out your calendar in one to two hour time blocks to accomplish your goals.

When you set the appointment on your calendar, I would _list exactly what you want to do. List what is needed to move the execution forward_. As an example, I would not set a time on your calendar that only says *Business Growth Time* because you will fall back into the "what should I do first" trap. Instead, set an appointment that says "Set up FB, LinkedIn, Google+ accounts. Add strong profiles with contact info." You see the difference? As soon as you sit down to grow your business on-purpose with appointments that speak to you, your execution becomes automatic.

Another _business execution tactic to explore is to work in "ferocious short bursts" to be more productive_. What I mean is this: within those one or two hour appointments you have blocked out, try working 50-minutes straight without any distractions whatsoever. Take a mandatory break for the last 10-minutes of that blocked hour and see how much more productive you will be. Trust me, it works really well.

I had the honor of speaking to 300-400 of my marketing peers on a marketers cruise. Everyone had a chance to speak on his or her specialty. The gentleman's name escapes me (shame on me), but he was a productivity specialist that consults with businesses big and small to help them maximize productivity. He said that if your take these short 50-minute ferocious bursts of execution and a mandatory ten-minute break to finish the hour, that in three short 50-minute session per day you can out-produce what most humans can do in a day and a half of work. That intrigued me, so I came home and filled my calendar... it worked ten times better than I had ever imagined! Adopt this policy to everything you want to execute. I promise you will be more productive and smash goals faster!

> **CEO Tip:** One positive business growth appointment on your calendar per week is worth 50+ positive business impacts on you business per year.

(FYI – I said 50 solid minutes without distractions, which includes closing down your e-mail, silencing your phone as you turn it face-down, and put all other work out of your sight. Find a place to work that minimizes human distraction, close down personal apps to work distraction free. No cheating! Your retirement plan depends on it!)

> # CEO Non-Negotiable: _Work in_
> _50-minute ferocious bursts of execution_
> _with mandatory ten-minute non-working_
> _breaks!_
>
> _(Your productivity will explode!)_

Another way to _increase execution_ of your business growth initiatives is to seek out a co-worker or peer as your _Accountability Partner_ to keep your high priority responsibilities at front-of-mind. If they are looking to accomplish some business goals or even workplace tasks, then you can be each other's accountability partner to push the ball forward. I would set monthly 30-minute in-person or phone appointments. Go over your accomplishments from the previous month and proclaim what four to eight items you both plan to execute in the coming month. Ask each other how the other person plans to accomplish their goals. Understand their approach and give advice if warranted, but be very clear on your intentions. Have weekly five to 15 minute calls to make sure each partner is on task and executing.

Accountability partnering works well to help push yourself and others to execute. If you have employees that need to execute, then try pairing them with accountability partners. As an example, I do some higher-end business coaching and paired up my business owners with other clients in the same growth program as weekly accountability partners. Then once a month we have a collective call to discuss that month's progress. You would be amazed how much more on-focus and productive the entrepreneurs were when they were being held accountable for their immediate action goals. It was amazing.

I would adopt this process into your execution plan to keep you on task and accountable. The really cool by-product of this method is receiving a fresh perspective from other business owners who do not have a stake in your business. A peer may see things that you can not. The feedback I have received was nothing short of amazing. (Disclaimer: I did tell each business owner to report to me via e-mail once a week if they had concerns about their accountability partner, so I could step in with some business tough-love.)

I love social pressure because it breeds execution. I'll help you if needed! *Don't be scared to be great, it is better to be scared of not being great!* You can also publicly post your weekly and monthly intentions for staff to see. If you are a one-man band, post it online for your peers to keep you on task. Bottom line here is that you need help to execute, so adopt policies to get more out of yourself. Your company deserves the best of you, so get out of your own way to deliver the best outcome possible!

The previous execution tips dovetail into the final practice I'm going to share with you. That is to set short goals for increased execution and focus. We've all been guilty of the "set it and forget it" trap, where you proclaim the goals and objectives for the year, only to file them away somewhere out of sight and get sucked right back into the day-to-day non-business growing vacuums. You know what I mean. Checking mindless e-mails and looking to see if everyone else is doing what they should be doing. Before you know it, eight to ten months have gone by and your goals are gathering dust. Now execution to complete these goals seems equivalent to climbing Mount Everest without gloves or shoes. A seemingly impossible task.

How can you solve this lack of execution? Set shorter, more executable goals. Create easier milestones to hit on the way to the overall goals for the year. Try setting 90-day goals with real execution plans broken out into smaller weekly tasks. It is human to look at big business goals like a mountain and let doubt creep into your business mind. That is why if you divide that mountain into smaller checkpoints along the way it is much easier to look up at the end of the journey and find your business on top of the mountain. My suggestion is to block out an hour next week and set four separate 90-day business initiative goals. Build these into your overall yearly goals to help your execution levels spike and let your business bank account be the biggest benefactor.

EXPLORE NEW INCOME STREAM OPPORTUNITIES

A business going from good to great can sometimes be as easy as exploring new income stream opportunities to add to your profit margins. As a business coach and consultant for years, it has become clear to me that most business owners do what they know and know what they do. In other words, they stick to their bread and butter business offerings.

Rarely do they venture outside of their business comfort zone to explore other income stream possibilities. Exploring these potential opportunities is a must for any 21st century business owner today. Why? Because technology has made it so easy to add an income stream and we are all ultra-connected within the Internet revolution. It should be crime not to at least explore the options to grow alternative income streams.

As I type this in my office, which I might add is in my house, I currently have 18 different incomes and prepared to add two more. This is not because I am a jack-of-all-trades. This is not because I am an expert at each of these income streams. It is because I devote real business brainpower uncovering the best possible solutions to consumer problems. I then look to streamline the best solution to that problem so it can run without me (or at least with as little of me as possible). This allows me to produce more income streams on-purpose! You can do the same!

I do the same process when consulting with entrepreneurs. I help them become the best solution in their niche by finding all possible solutions, and streamlining the best solutions to run the business efficiently as well as profitably. Then we look to automate it (if possible) or train a protégé so it can run independently to free the owner up to do more income producing activities. Your business should be no different. Let's explore the business income possibilities together.

AFFILIATES

The first logical step down this path is to _look and see what products and services are good compliments to your business offerings. Investigate if there is a way to become affiliated with the right partner_. As an example, let's say your core business is dry cleaning services. You have cultivated a loyal customer base as their dry cleaning solution. Isn't it safe to say that you're probably the first to know if the customer's shirt or pants need some seamstress attention? If that is the case, then why are you not already affiliated with one of the ten seamstress service companies in your area? As an affiliate, you should get ten percent of the revenue generated from your referrals to their business. Furthermore, I'm quite certain that their seamstress clients need your services too. Set up the same referral affiliate commission with the seamstress to incentivize them to send business to you. A true win-win relationship.

Depending on your business offerings, you can also *turn all of your customers into your affiliates as well*. They can either get free offerings from you for referring new customers or you can compensate them fiscally for their referrals. This is a great way to grow your business and to strengthen customer loyalty to your brand.

My suggestion to you is to think about what other services go hand-in-hand with your products. Create affiliate relationships with these complimentary companies to earn even more income. Set a goal to build three to five new income funnels that fit your business offerings. With today's e-commerce sites that turn you into instant affiliates, the possibilities are virtually endless.

To see some e-commerce and affiliate solutions visit affiliatebreakdown.com, which gives you reviews of some of the biggest affiliate e-commerce solutions. It makes your choices easier on which products and services to add as new income streams.

(A quick note to add here: I'm speaking of online affiliations simply because they are easy. That does not mean I am adverse to good old signed documents and handshakes! Go out and create any and all new income stream relationships! Okay! Got it? Good!)

CLIENT SHARING

Another potential revenue stream to consider is *client-sharing promotions with complimentary companies that are open to cross-promotion*. They can share your offerings to their customer base via e-mail or offline mailing. You can do the same for them. They can do an online presentation to their customers about your products and services to produce sales. I've used this online presentation avenue numerous times to sell my real estate automation software and shared commissions with the person hosting the presentation. Hopefully I'm expanding your business mind here. The possibilities are endless.

> **CEO RESOURCE:** Free online conferencing for online meetings. www.join.me or www.gotomeeting.com

BUY ACCESS TO SOMEONE'S LIST

A different twist along the lines of client sharing is *paying a flat fee for a one-time promotion to your target audience via an affiliate*. Most of the time they are called *media-buys* where you contact a list broker and simply approach a big player in your business space. They have thousands and thousands of contacts and will negotiate a flat fee to send a one-time message with your best marketing pitch and hooks to see how many new clients you can grab.

A friend of mine does this and he can fetch anywhere from $2,000 all the way up to $15,000 an e-mail, depending on the audience. You may be thinking that is a lot. It is a lot of money, but what if you sell your product for $1,000 and it goes to 100,000 of your perfect prospects? He has a mega-loyal following. If he says your product is a "must-see" is it worth paying for the endorsement if you get 85 sales from it? The answer is a resounding, YES!

Is your mind racing yet? Just one e-mail from the right person with a strong connection to their list and your sales could explode! Honestly, the only thing that is even in question here is, "How good is your marketing message and call-to-action?" If it is good, then you can be swimming in new business income by tomorrow morning. I would devote some time to reading about "Media Buying" and "List Buying" as strategies to develop some new favorite income stream opportunities.

SPEAKING

Get paid to speak. Yes, you! Whether or not you are an expert or working to become one, you should be getting paid to speak. I've heard that public speaking in the second biggest fear for most people. The first fear is death. (Don't know if it is true or not!) Regardless, if you create a PowerPoint and speak on a subject that you are passionate about, then you can start to earn income by teaching and informing others. You can do it for free if it is going to get you business. However, the better you become at speaking and the more expert information that you provide; you can get paid to speak while generating new clients as well.

CONSULTING

For those that already know me, they have heard me say 100 times, *"Back up the value truck!"* I say it in meetings, consultations, trainings, and speeches. If you are really good at something, you need to share it with others. Turn that into massive income for you business. The key is to give away your best value, or in other words, "Give away the farm!" Don't hold back because you will leave them wanting even more of you and your company.

When they want more, get paid for it as a consultant. Experts get paid for their time. I always say not to hold back trade secrets (to an extent of course. Keep a little bit behind the curtain.) because if you deliver massive value, then the benefactors receiving it will logically think, "If s/he is giving me this unbelievably amazing stuff, then what else am I missing?" Rather than trying to do what you do, they will just ask you to do it for them. Help others and get paid to do it!

FRANCHISE

The last new income stream to explore is to _turn your process into a franchise model and get royalties and franchise set-up fees_. This isn't for everyone that reads this, but it might be for you. If you have a new business, a new way of doing things that is unique, or if you have a unique business model, then you may have the foundation to franchise it. Build around your great idea and share the vision with others (after non-disclosures, of course). When they agree with your business model, look to franchise it with them and then sit back and collect income.

CONCLUSION

As you can see, _my vision for your business is bigger_. You may think that you are light years away from a couple of these income possibilities, but I promise you that you are not. I said it before and I'll say it again: the only thing stopping you is you! The only thing keeping you from beating your competition is exploration and execution. I've already given you a blueprint for maximizing execution. Exploring new income possibilities is just one more way to build a bigger business on-purpose. Your business can spit out income like a well-oiled income-machine! Bring in a consultant, a mentor, and a partner and take action to springboard your business income to the next level.

CEO ACTIVITY: List Five Potential Complimentary Income Offerings

- List the various offerings that can compliment your business offerings.
- List where you plan to search for these complimentary offerings.
- Block out the search on your calendar.

Make calls and set one-on-one appointments to strike deals with affiliates for complimentary service offerings. These win-win relationships put more money in your pocket as well as your affiliate partner's pocket.

Chapter 10:

Business Legacy

TURN SUCCESS INTO SUCCESSION!

The crowning achievement on your path to building a bigger business is the moment your hard work delivers an unstoppable business legacy that will produce income for the next generation and beyond. "*A bigger on-purpose business has legacy already woven into its fabric.*" It has leverage, multiple streams of income, tested marketing ready for the next battle, perfect customer persona in its sight, documented processes, clear business vision, massive online presence, the right people in place, and an On-Purpose CEO that learned to ask for help and got out of their own way.

That business is not an accident. That is a business anyone would want. This chapter addresses business succession. We will discuss what you want to protect as we finalize your fastest path to retirement and lay the framework to leave a lasting business legacy.

We've all heard the saying "He/she is bigger than life." We all know that statement is not true. You can't be bigger than life, but your business can! If you've followed the purposeful path and built your best "bigger business blueprint," then you've built a business that we can safely attach some legacy pillars to for business succession.

"You can't be bigger than life, but your business legacy can!"

– Jason Palliser

HANDING OVER THE KEYS TO THE CASTLE!

Throughout our journey, you've discovered the keys to a profitable modern business. You've purposefully followed the bigger business blueprint path and unlocked the castle. Your business is now battle-tested. You've become the executioner and slayed your competition. There is peace in the business kingdom you've worked so hard to build. You've leveraged your way into a more profitable business, which is nimble and ready to stand up to the competition. You can say that you've built something that is bigger than you.

As you are inching closer to handing over the keys to the castle we need to make sure you hand over the keys to a healthy business-kingdom. We don't want to hand the keys to the kingdom to your chosen successor(s) only to be slaughtered by the competition. A prudent business king/queen would first build out his/her succession plan deliberately in order to bid the business kingdom a proper farewell. It is time to pass the keys over when you've reached your income goals and you've built a business that can grow on its own. But, we need to protect what you've built.

PROTECTING THE KINGDOM

Just like a king or queen protects their kingdom like it is their precious child, you need to do the same with your business. Working hard to build your business is a purposeful and emotional process. Being separated from something you've worked so hard on is almost like the feeling of leaving your child. It is hard to do. As you prepare to pass your business-baby to a new caretaker, you want to make sure it is protected and taken care of. You also need to protect yourself.

You can accomplish this by executing documents that protect the business infrastructure (rules and regulations), protect the business value, delineate business vision, state your intentions and expectations, and safeguard the transfer of power (ownership) to help pave the way for the business successors. As we begin to break this down, it is imperative to note that, while these are future agenda items for you, the future is now. Building protection into your business is not a later thing, it is a now thing. You do not know what tomorrow brings, so it is better to be prepared. Putting protections in place can help preserve the integrity of the business versus leaving the kingdom up for grabs. Let's deliver the keys to your protected kingdom.

LIFE INSURANCE

Let's face it. We truly don't know what tomorrow will bring, so be an On-Purpose CEO and protect against that risk with life insurance. Please note, I am simply asking you to consider purchasing life insurance for the "Key Members" of your business. If they were tragically gone tomorrow, it would undoubtedly affect the operation or valuation of the business. If you have life insurance on a key member that passes away, the insurance proceeds may give you the capital you need to keep the company running until a suitable replacement is located. The insurance increases the chances of the business surviving when an unfortunate situation arises.

The bottom line is that the company suffers when a key member is removed from the mix and you need to plan for it. If purchased properly, you can build tax-deferred cash value in the company through the policy and that can reduce the taxable income of the company. So plan wisely.

OPERATING AGREEMENT AND ARTICLES OF ORGANIZATION

(**Disclaimer**: *I am not an attorney, so before you do anything with respect to business planning documents, consult an attorney. This content is for educational purposes only.*)

Additional documents vital to protecting your business are articles of organization and operating agreements. These are the core documents from which most businesses are run by placing policies, procedures and responsibilities for all interested parties within the business. They are used to officially delineate the way the business matters are to be handled and used from time to time as the benchmark for settling disputes.

They spell out ownership interests. They convey business names and owners to local, state, and federal institutions. You need the organizational documents in-hand to open up business bank accounts, to start collecting income, and make deposits from customers.

The operating agreement may establish company cash disbursement percentages on a monthly basis to protect the company against one or more person draining cash from the company. It may also establish voting rights in the event there are differing opinions on a business matter. It looks to resolve any business deadlock issues, create standard practices, codes of conduct policies, and penalties on voting said points.

An operating agreement item for any business with two or

more persons as owners, is the _Triggering Events_ article that determines how the sale of the company will be handled. This is critical for your business to have or put in place in order to avoid bad business situations down the road. One big triggering event that surprises partnerships is the death of a partner and what happens with the business if one of you passes away. If you don't have a clause and your partner passes away, then you may be stuck with running the business with their spouse or children.

Laws vary by state, but if you approach this strategically, you can buy (for example) one million dollars of life insurance on your partner and make the business the beneficiary. Let's say they pass away and you use $150,000 to hire a serviceable replacement for your partner and you have $850,000 thousand left over to buy out the spouse. Also it is important to note that if you set up a death sales trigger clause that allows you to buy out any interest your partner had, then the spouse does not have a say in whether or not you buy them out of the business. I sincerely hope this sounds like an On-Purpose CEO to-do item for you.

Your documents can also state what valuation model will be used for the company when someone internally or externally wants to buy the business. This is critical to try to reduce (and hopefully) eliminate guesswork when it comes to arriving at a business valuation and business sale number. Otherwise, you can end up in a business sale deadlock simply because two sides of the negotiation are using their own method to find the company value.

These documents are critical to make sure you protect the integrity of you business now and in the future. Take the time to bulletproof this part of your business and eliminate any partnership guesswork that may happen in the future.

PERSONAL SUCCESSION PLANNING

Independent of your business documents is your personal planning and wishes delineated through a trust document. You can leave your business and assets to whomever you choose. You can split it up if you choose. You can put it in a trustee's hands for them to carry out your wishes, thus ensuring others don't misuse the opportunities you are leaving them.

You may want to set it up inside a living trust. This is independent of your business documents and further spells out exactly what you want to be done with your business for our purposes here. The possibilities are endless. As an example, you may want to hand the business over to your children, but you want the most financially savvy one to be the tiebreaker when any disagreements occur. Depending on the business documents in place, you may delineate your exact intentions here. You may want them to run the business for ten years before they can sell it and you can add that as a stipulation as well.

The fact is, you've worked (or are working) hard to get to this point and the last thing you want is to build a profitable business, just to have it torn apart after you pass your legacy on to your successors. The key here is to plan for it now so that you can wake up each day knowing the business will have your purposeful path laid out, giving your successor(s) the best chance to carry on your business legacy the way you intend. No accidents, no guesswork, just on-purpose legacy succession!

BIGGER BUSINESS KEY

"True wealth is not just the income you receive; it is in the business legacy you leave!"

You've arrived! You have what most competitors can only dream of: a bigger business blueprint. You've gone from customer to closing. You've woven winning business non-negotiables into the fabric of your business. You've put the plan in place to meet the world where they live (online) to maximize your exposure and opportunity. You've shifted your On-Purpose CEO focus to modernizing your business. You achieved hands-free business building and can boast growth through trackable marketing efforts. You've eliminated guesswork and are creating higher profits.

You've documented your philosophy, approach, and practices to allow independent growth. You've become an executioner that embodies razor sharp focus to work "on" your business rather than "in" your business. You've become a more valuable business with clear brand awareness and game-changing Unique Selling Propositions that command marketplace attention. You've successfully discovered the way to build a wall around your perfect customer persona that shields your new customers from the cold wind of the competition.

Your business has never been more poised for purposeful growth and leverage, unlocking the door to more streams of income that can and will march you towards the retirement finish line. You have the blueprint to implement your growth goals and have planted the seed, which will provide wealth and income for generations to come.

You have the keys to the castle and your modern business is your kingdom. As you'll begin to see, true wealth does not just reside in the income you've received, it comes full-circle in the legacy you leave. So embrace the Business-Nirvana you're marching towards, develop your best income-producing machine using these principles, and not only leave your legacy, leave your undeniable On-Purpose CEO mark on today's modern business landscape.

CEO RESOURCE: Business Bulletproofing and Succession Planning Request:

BiggerBusinessBlueprint.com/BizBulletproof

Conclusion

"Knowledge is Great, Execution is Greater!"

— Jason Palliser

If you've made it this far, then you are what I call a "two percent-er!" You are one of the few that will not worry about what isn't happening in your business; instead you are seeking to work on your business to create the business vision your desire. If you've participated with me throughout the journey, then let me be the first to tell you that _your CEO Value has never been higher_.

The knowledge you possess is an immeasurable competitive edge over the competition. But, I need to warn you that massive knowledge is also a double-edged sword, from the standpoint of putting the knowledge to purposeful use. If you have the knowledge to build a bigger business but you don't use it, then instead of slicing the competition, you may be cutting yourself instead.

When I consult with my entrepreneurs, I always tell them it will not be the business owner with the highest IQ that will build the bigger business. The business owner that takes their knowledge and executes it will be the winner every time. The moral of the story here is that "Knowledge is great, execution is greater!" On-Purpose CEOs execute their vision and let the blueprint they create become the income-producing guide to not only meet their business goals, but exceed them. _The only purpose for this chapter is to help you organize your new knowledge and skill sets and build your tangible bigger business blueprint_. Let's start putting the plans together.

EXECUTE!

The best way to build your _bigger business blueprint_ is to grab all of your notes from each chapter, grab all of your activity collateral, and your business honesty score test questions. List them all out in one document or mind-map (www.xmind. net). I find mind maps easiest, but it's up to you. Anyway, get them all in one spot for you and your team to view (if you have a team of course). The next step it to prioritize them in order of importance to you.

1. Grab all of your notes, activity collateral and BHS test questions and put them in a document or mind map.
2. Prioritize them in order of importance, according to you.
3. Ask yourself if you can attach leverage to each action item and list it next to the task for later use.
4. Ask yourself if you can automate any of your business action items and list _how_ next to the action item for later use.
5. Add a teammate to each action item to help or manage that action item for later delegation
6. Finally, Take a break and walk away! Come back later for the final step to world class execution!

> **CEO TIP:** Just because everything is in front of you does not mean you have to do "everything!" An On-Purpose CEO knows Rome wasn't built in a day and your most profitable business will not be either.

Your next step is to look at each item and ask yourself if you can attach leverage resources to it. (Yo, CEO! Refer back to the chapter on leverage and attach one of them to the task). Trying to make your life easier here. Ask, "Can I automate it?" The big key here is to start attaching leverage pieces like a mad scientist. A few leverage pieces if you can. Later you can decide which is the best choice to help you execute like an organized world champion.

The last element to add to the master execution document is a team assignment. If you are a "one-man-band," then it looks like you will be attached to everything, which is fine. On the same map or document you are creating, attach the person that will be spearheading that task/element of your business execution plan. Take note that I am asking you to take a mandatory 30-minute break once you've reached this spot for a reason.

Stepping away for a moment will help you clear your CEO mind that is swimming in a soup bowl of initiatives and tasks. I promise when you come back to the blueprint it will not look the same. Your subconscious will have resolved some of the tweaking to the plan it wanted to do while your were working on just getting it out of your head.

SHARE YOUR VISION

Now that you've spilled your bigger business blueprint vision out of your head, it is time to share the vision. The more you share it, the bigger the vision becomes. Your business has to be bigger than just you. Sharing it is the way to make it happen. Share it with your team, your business partner, your business consultant, your business mentor, your sphere of influence, your spouse, and yourself. Yes, I said you.

Print it out. Hold it in your hands. It is tangible. Look at it and smile! You've done something most businesses never do. You put your future and business growth vision in writing! W-I-N-N-I-N-G!

The faster you make it tangible, the faster the vision becomes reality. It is easier for you and for other people to get behind what they hear, but also what they can see and feel. You've set the stage! Now it is time to perform!

My Greatest Gift Of All To You... A Bone-Crushing Execution Plan!

TRADING 30 FOR 180

Now that you have a blueprint in front of you, it is time to take your execution to a whole new level. How do we do this critical step that keeps most entrepreneurs at the starting gate? We go into execution-overdrive by "_Trading 30 for 180!_"

You would trade $30 for $180 dollars wouldn't you? Of course you would! It is a no-brainer, right? I'll bet that in your mind you already handed over the $30 and the execution was made on almost autopilot. _Trading 30 for 180_ is exactly the process you need to do with your business action items list.

Trading 30 for 180 is the process I crafted to help my consulting clients get out of their lack-of-execution trap. _Trading 30 for 180 is simply the process of making you sit down without any distractions. Take 30 minutes to add your prioritized blueprint action-items into your calendar in weekly tasks for the next six months or 180 days. Hence, "Trading 30 For 180!"_

"The Best CEO Execution Is Action Planning In Motion!"

Mastering this process is literally where you can set yourself apart from the rest of the business world. "*Trading 30 For 180*" is the process of putting your execution plans in motion and kick starting your bigger business, with weekly finish lines to consistently keep you in the winner's circle.

It is an unfortunate reality that most businesses fail. The real truth is that they never get out of the starting gate. They do not have an actionable blueprint and they definitely do not have an execution process to turn the blueprint into their bigger business vision.

From this point forward the most critical aspect of your business growth success is executing the plan that you can print and hold in your hands. Your plan is real! It is not just a bunch of accidental CEO thoughts. The ONLY thing holding you back from becoming the biggest business that you can imagine while blowing the doors off of the competition is *purposeful execution*.

TIMELINE

Block CEO Business Building on your calendar in one or two hour increments to knock out your blueprint. If you have teammates, then have them do the same right next to you. Remember what I said from before; don't just add an appointment to your calendar that says "Business Building." If I ever see that on your calendar I am going to swoop in on you with a different type of execution plan that you probably don't want (sorry, had to make sure I get my point across clearly). Instead, block calendar appointments that have specific task like the following:

Week 1

- Tuesday 9am -11am: Take my Top 10 things to know

about my business and turn them into e-mails for my follow up campaigns. | Who – Jerry | Resource: Use ScriptDoll.com for help |

- Thursday 10am – 11am: Decide which CRM to use and watch four tutorial videos on how to add e-mail campaigns for customer follow up. Set up first campaign! |Who – Me | Resources: Check out Constant Contact, ZOHO, Infusionsoft and decide!

Week 2

- Monday 3pm – 5pm: Copy and paste my Top 10 e-mails into my follow up campaign engine and add my customer contacts to the engine and hit "Go" |Who – Sally | Resource: Marketing Word Doc where Top 10 is saved
- Friday 12pm – 2pm: Type out my Top 10 FAQs and add them to my website | Who – Sales Team and Me | Resource: Save to company "Marketing" Word Doc

Week 3

- Tuesday 8am – 10am: 1. Set up an account on www.textbroker.com and post an ad there to help me write a business mission statement and welcome video script for my business. (*Note, this will probably take you 10 minutes, so you have lots of time to accomplish another blueprint item.*) 2. Set up a www.fiverr.com account and search for a video expert to make my video for $5
- Friday 2pm – 3pm: Set up Free 1-on-1 VA Interview at www.leveragemate.com and hire them to build my Facebook Business Page, Twitter Profile and LinkedIn Groups

Week 4

- Monday 10am – 12pm: 1. Get my business listed in all of

the online directories. |Resource: www.knowem.com |
2. Check out www.hootsuite.com and www.ifttt.com
to set up accounts |Then go to www.YouTube.com for
"Hootsuite" and "If This Then That" videos and watch
them to see how I can use them.

- Thursday 11am – 1pm: Brainstorm on coming up with
new Unique Selling Propositions. |Who – Me and
Team| Resource: Add them to "USP" Word Doc and
add them to your marketing pieces to see which ones
spike sales.

And so on.... You get the gist, correct? _Set real calendar
appointments that are action orientated_. Remember, if you
knock out just two items a week, you will accomplish over 50
business building items in less than six months!

Please note, I suggest scheduling two appointments a week,
but you can set more. I do not have the benefit of knowing
your business yet, so I don't know your timeline. You may have
a team helping you and can leverage your way to success!

The point here is to _put your execution on autopilot for the
next six months_, so you don't even have to think after you've
completed your trading 30 for 180 tasks. You just wake up,
look at the appointment actions and execute to completion.
You might as well add your retirement party to your calendar
because if you follow this trading 30 for 180 process, then it is
coming towards you like a freight train!

CEO RESOURCE: Execution Planning

BiggerBusinessBlueprint.com/ExecutionHelp

FRONT OF MIND

Take things even one step further inside the purposeful execution theme. _I am not asking, I am commanding that you list all of the CEO Tips and Non-Negotaibles you've learned. Print all of your tips/standard practices, and run to FedEx to laminate them._ Make three or four copies of them and display them wherever you sit to accomplish work every day. Keep one by your laptop at home. Display your Business Non-Negotiables at work for everyone to see. Put one in your car or wherever else you think you need it, so that it is _a constant reminder of how you do what you do and how you are getting there._

Pretty simple... print, laminate and display!

**Your Bigger Business Blueprint is crystal clear**! The final step to your bigger business blueprint to produce more income with less effort is to **_execute_**. If you've followed the blueprint, then you cleared the way for total execution. If you've followed the process without deviation and machine-like devotion, then the stage is set for massive performance.

FINAL NOTE

Now when you swing your business sword, you're cutting down the competition. They can't escape. Your business, brand and vision are everywhere. Your reward at the end of the Bigger Business Blueprint journey is a business that grabs marketshare, grows with less effort, and spits out new income streams _on-purpose_!

My hope is that my _tireless pursuit for business perfection_, stemming from all the entrepreneurs I have touched, has imprinted into your On-Purpose CEO mind a better way to build a Bigger Business Blueprint! And... that in some way I get the chance (and honor) to be there with you to celebrate your business wins and victories that push you towards your retirement party. (*We all know that I love a good party! Well you may not have known, but now you do!*)

"Your options for business growth are now virtually endless because your success is no longer an accident; it is on-purpose. Covet your bigger business blueprint! Protect it! Automate it so your business not only meets the demands of the Modern 21st Century Business World; it transcends it!"

*And in a word, **Execute**!*

Your Tireless Business Growth Partner,
Bigger Business Blueprint
Jason Palliser

Jason@goseejason.com

CEO RESOURCE: Contact me for a consultation

BiggerBusinessBlueprint.com/ConsultingHelp

TESTIMONIALS:

"I did a class with you a year or so ago and I wanted to let you know I really got a lot out of the class! I still use your non-negotiables daily!" – Kevin Flaherty

"I really enjoyed your class and am grateful for all of the tools you shared! Elite Legacy is lucky to have you teaching!!" – Selma K. Thompson

"I took Jason's marketing class in Orlando Florida, and it was the best thing I have done to date to improve my business. I have been using pay per click ads for a while now, and I haven't had much success with it, but while sitting in Jason's class I made some changes to the ads with Jason's material, and that night I had over 17 incoming phone calls and got one property under contract. I also got $200 of free credit for advertising from google because of how successful the ads were. That was only a small part of what Jason teaches about marketing, and everything you learn is going to drive you more leads, create more success, and overall bring more money to your business. If you apply what he teaches you will see it start to work immediately, and will always beat your competition." - Michael DeVault

"I've been trying to catch you at this symposium, but wanted to let you know that using Ifttt.com has really helped! I scrape a lot of sites with it and get notifications on my phone in seconds. I am always the first to call and start a relationship!

Last month we paid x, sold the next day for 2x and owner financed it for them at 9%! All because I was the first to call and the owner liked that!

Thank you!" -Julie Cowan, M.Ed Educational Therapist/ Professional Level

"Wow seriously appreciated Jason and beyond my expectations. Thanks for providing so much added value!" – Ken Krongard

"I was thinking back about the weekend and to say it was overwhelming was an understatement. I didn't bust out in tears, but I can say I felt a tear roll down my face. Wow!" – Paul Warnagiris

"Speaking with you has helped me to move to the next level!" – Grant Michael Phillips

"Now we have 40 thousand followers on Twitter with squeeze pages getting us leads everyday, we can't thank you enough man." - Kevin Flaherty

"Jason is the one from whom I have learned 99% of the marketing for my businesses as well the "Value Principle." He is extremely intelligent and down-to-earth. Also, he is a Value Leader and a great friend." – Mac Mirza

"Incredible class in L.A. last week! Thanks for splitting my brain!" – Nicole D. Martinez

"Your training was fantastic!!! This is going to help out BIG

TIME with different businesses ventures I'm involved with. I had no idea how to market with social media even though I am a software engineer." – Nabahwaya Courten

CEO RESOURCES (MENTIONED IN THE BOOK):

- Virtual Assistant Leverage: www.leveragemate.com - Cheap Assistant Help
- Productivity Tool: www.timedoctor.com - Tracks your time on the computer
- Mind Mapping Software: www.xmind.net, www.mindjet.com
- Going Paperless Software: www.hellosign.com
- Shared Appointment Calendar: www.youcanbookme.com
- Targeted Data Lists: www.listsource.com, www.listability.com, www.melissadata.com
- Competitor Research: www.whatrunswhere.com
- Company Naming Resource: www.namingforce.com
- Social Media Scheduling Tool: www.hootsuite.com
- Logo Design Contest: www.99designs.com
- Professional Writing Cheap: www.textbroker.com
- Website Themes Cheap: www.templatemonster.com
- Online Directory Placement: www.knowem.com
- Automated Sales Copy Writing: www.scriptdoll.com
- Free Video Screen Capture: www.jingproject.com
- Blast Text Message Software: www.sendhub.com
- Automated Lead Generation: www.ifttt.com - Recipes
- Automated YouTube.com Leads: www.tubetoolbox.com
- Online Press Releases: www.prlog.org, www.prweb.com
- Buying Domain Names: www.godaddy.com
- Bandit Signs: www.banditsigns.com, www.dircheapsigns.com
- Make Easy Money With T-Shirt Ideas: www.teespring.com
- Hiring and Employee Resource: www.rework.withgoogle.com
- Free Online Meeting Software: www.join.me

BIGGER BUSINESS BLUEPRINT NOTABLE QUOTES:

1. Build An On-Purpose Business! – Jason Palliser

2. To know your business, is to grow your business! – Jason Palliser

3. Every business can improve! – Jason Palliser

4. Knowledge is great, execution is greater! – Jason Palliser

5. I'm not here to deliver information. I'm here to command business transformation! – Jason Palliser

6. Be an On-Purpose CEO! – Jason Palliser

7. Winning CEOs always look to refine their process. It makes cents! – Jason Palliser

8. To grow you need to get out of your own way! – Jason Palliser

9. Your business without proper advertising is like winking at a girl in the dark. You know what you are doing, but nobody else does! – Stuart Henderson

10. If you don't manage your brand, someone will do it for you, and that somebody will likely be your competitor. – Donald Trump

11. Your brand is everything, so defend it! – Jason Palliser

12. Find your brand position and build a fortress around it! – Jason Palliser

13. Brand building is not a part time job! – Jason Palliser

14. Never ignore your happy customers for they are your best sales team! – Unknown

15. In today's online consumer jungle, interaction is the key to success! – Jason Palliser

16. Growing through social media is the "no gas money spent program!" – Jason Palliser

17. Your business isn't in your office; it lives in the minds you meaningfully touch! – Unknown

18. Privately connect with your customers well; they'll praise you publicly! - Unknown

19. Everyone can _have_ a business, but not everyone can be _in_ business! – Jason Palliser

20. Great execution is the ultimate differentiator. – Margaret Molloy

21. Circle the wagons around your new customers! You worked hard to get them, so don't forget them! - Jason Palliser

22. Marketing is no longer about the stuff that you make, but about the stories you tell. – Seth Godin

23. If you can't explain it to a six-year old, you don't know it yourself.– Albert Einstein

24. 8 out of 10 consumers will read the headline copy, but only 2 out of 10 will read the rest! – CopyBlogger

25. Headlines are worth 90% of the advertising dollar! – David Ogilvy

26. Marketing's job is never done. It is about perpetual motion. We must continue to innovate everyday. – Beth Comstock

27. You want to beat your competition? Then become a marketing mad-scientist! – Jason Palliser

28. Tweaking is peaking! – Jason Palliser

29. No one is stopping you, but you! – Unknown

30. For you to decide to not get social with your business is like purposefully ignoring ¾ of the world as a business decision! – Jason Palliser

31. Not getting your customers involved in your business is a business-sin! – Jason Palliser

32. It takes 20 years to build a reputation and five minutes to ruin it. If you think about that, you'll do things differently. - Warren Buffet

33. The hours that ordinary people waste, extraordinary people leverage. – Robin Sharma

34. Leverage! You either have it or you don't! – Jason Palliser

35. Trying to grow a business without the key component of leverage is like farming without seeds. You can stir up a lot of dirt, but in the end you're still left with dirt! – Jason Palliser

36. If college students have to do an internship before they graduate, why aren't they working for you? – Jason Palliser

37. No one knows more than everyone in business, therefore seeking outside help is the mark of a truly smart business mind! – Jason Palliser

38. Work on your "E's" in the right order! Earnings over Ease! Big payoff items first! – Jason Palliser

39. If you want to kill the competition, become an executioner! – Jason Palliser

40. Turn success into succession! – Jason Palliser

41. You can't be bigger than life, but your business legacy can! – Jason Palliser

42. Trading 30 for 180! – Jason Palliser

43. The best CEO execution is action planning in motion! – Jason Palliser

ABOUT THE AUTHOR

Jason Palliser, a St. Louis Missouri native, has been speaking and training for over 15 years and has touched thousands of entrepreneurs with his business growth approaches. Building bigger business blueprints by infusing innovative leverage principals into each entrepreneur's growth execution plan is the hallmark of his signature approach.

Palliser's mastery of the business growth process has landed him on some of the largest leadership stages in the nation impacting thousands. His accomplishments include a degree from the University Of Missouri in Personal Finance, Top 100 Originators in the U.S.A. for closed transactions per year (Mortgage Originator Magazine), Trainer of the Year for Rich Dad Education, Million Dollar Sales Award from Speaking Empire and more.

Besides impacting every entrepreneur he touches, his other passions include football, racquetball, baseball, quests for new innovation, travel, pranks, movies, family, and much more. He is always looking for the next challenge. Solving new challenges daily is what drives his entrepreneurial mind. Ultimately, his mission is to leave each business owner he touches with a bigger and better business blueprint.

Speaking & Consulting Clients Include:

World Care Alliance
Elite Legacy Education
Medical Management Services
Zurixx
Southern Bowl
Flipping Formula
Revergence Healthcare LLC
Lifestyles Unlimited
Investor Boardroom
Expand The Business
Prospect Master
Sales Mastery
Rich Dad Education
United Labor Benefits
Affinity Real Estate Solutions
Planet Rent To Own
Metrocities Mortgage
Secured Investment Corp
Dutchman Realty
Lifeoniare
Real Market Masters
REI Blackbook
Massas
United Country
Note Worthy
Turtle Creek Pub & Grill
Giesler Sports World Wide
South Side Investment
Equity Trust
And countless small-business entrepreneurs

CPSIA information can be obtained
at www.ICGtesting.com
Printed in the USA
FFOW01n1702280616
25459FF

9 780991 041671